EDITORIAL
Editor Dave Stevenson
Managing Editor Priti Patel
Design & Layout Heather Reeves

LICENSING & SYNDICATION
Licensing Carlotta Serantoni,
carlotta_serantoni@dennis.co.uk,
+44 20 7907 6550
Syndication Anj Dosaj-Halai,
Anj_Dosaj-Halai@dennis.co.uk,
+44 20 7907 6132

ADVERTISING & MARKETING
MagBook Account Manager
Katie Wood +44 20 7907 6689
Senior MagBook Executive
Matt Wakefield +44 20 7907 6617
Digital Production Manager
Nicky Baker +44 20 7907 6056
MagBook Manager
Dharmesh Mistry +44 20 7907 6100
Marketing Executive
Paul Goodhead +44 20 7907 6012

MANAGEMENT +44 20 7907 6000
Managing Director John Garewal
Deputy Managing Director Tim Danton
MD of Advertising Julian Lloyd-Evans
Newstrade Director David Barker
Chief Operating Officer Brett Reynolds
Group Finance Director Ian Leggett
Chief Executive James Tye
Chairman Felix Dennis

Printed by
BGP, Bicester, Oxfordshire
The paper used within this MagBook is
produced from sustainable fibre, manufactured
by mills with a valid chain of custody.
ISBN 1-78106-032-0

Thanks to The British Wildlife Centre,
Surrey www.camerasunderwater.co.uk
Scuba Junkie, Borneo

Letter from the editor

Starting out in photography is tough. Determining what all
the buttons, dials and wheels on your camera are for takes
long enough; uncovering the secrets of good exposure and
composition will set you back a few more weeks; the learning
curve for taking great photographs is never-ending.

This book is designed to make that curve a little shallower.
Instead of simply defining technical terms, we're leading by
example. Each page features a photograph that anyone can
take, given the right technique, approach and, in some cases,
equipment. Alongside the photo, you'll find a step-by-step
guide that explains how to turn the subject in front of you
into a stunning image.

We've covered the most popular genres of photography.
If you're a regular at your local wildlife park, turn to p46 to
find out how to make the most of the opportunities there –
and even how to make fences disappear from your images.
If you find yourself the designated photographer at family
gatherings, p22 and p24 will help you keep group photos
interesting and your shots of children fresh. For the
abstract-minded, chapter 11 should help produce photographs
that do justice to your imagination.

There's one piece of advice that overrides all others:
jump in. Take your camera with you everywhere and keep a
constant lookout for the best position or the angle nobody
else has thought of. Technical knowledge is one thing, but
it's a sense of adventure and creativity that produces the
most spectacular images. With this book nestled in your
camera bag, authoritative help will always be at hand; the
rest is up to you.

DAVE STEVENSON www.davestevenson.co.uk

CONTENTS

004 Technical
006   What the shutter does
008   What the aperture does
010   How to use ISO
012   Navigating your camera's controls
014   Notes on flash
016   Choosing memory cards

018 Portraits
020   In the bag
022   Group portraits
024   Perfect photos of children
026   Taking shots of individuals
030   Enhanced lighting

032 Landscapes
034   In the bag
036   Shooting at dawn
038   Using unusual frame sizes
040   Using graduated filters
042   Using a tilt-shift lens
044   Maximise depth of field & sharpness

046 Wildlife
048   In the bag
050   Wildlife from afar
052   Getting good shots at the zoo
056   Shooting garden birds
058   Capturing movement
060   Using autofocus

062 Architecture
064   In the bag
066   Shooting from high up
068   Taking photos of tall buildings
070   Adding impact using black & white

072 Winter
074   In the bag
076   Getting exposure correct in the snow
078   Taking care of your gear in the cold
080   Correcting white balance

082 Sport
084   In the bag
086   How to show movement
088   Find a good position
090   Get your timing right

026

058

066

086

092 Indoor
094   In the bag
096   Using light indoors
098   Using ISO
100   Good party photography
101   Photographing action indoors
102   Taking photos at gigs
104   Still life

106 Night
108   In the bag
110   Using exposure to create light trails
112   Using tripods
114   Shooting handheld

116 Underwater
118   In the bag
120   Using underwater housings
122   Editing underwater photos
124   Using lenses underwater
126   Backscatter & underwater lighting

128 Special Effects
130   In the bag
132   Water droplets
134   Flower close-ups
138   Ink in water
140   Indoor light trails
142   Mist effects

144 Printing
146   How to choose your printer
148   Understanding inks
150   Understanding paper
152   Processing your image
154   Cropping & resolution
156   Professional printing
158   Framing & mounting

160 Glossary

110

116

132

TECHNICAL

It's entirely possible for someone who has never handled a camera before to take a brilliant shot – modern cameras are extremely intelligent. However, the less you understand about the technicalities of how a camera works and how to set it up, the less chance you have of marrying up the shot in your head with the resulting image.

It sounds complex: shutter speeds, aperture sizes, ISO and f-stops can all be tricky to master, and in the early days you'll make more mistakes than masterpieces. Likewise, learning how each camera setting affects every other setting can take some time to sink in.

But persevere! With the knowledge you'll pick up in the following pages – plus plenty of practice – the key concepts of photography will start to fall into place. Before long you'll find yourself instinctively balancing your camera's settings, thinking in stops, and unconsciously measuring how strong the light is and where it's coming from before you even put your eye to the viewfinder.

006 What the shutter does

008 What the aperture does

010 How to use ISO

012 Navigating your camera's controls

014 Notes on flash

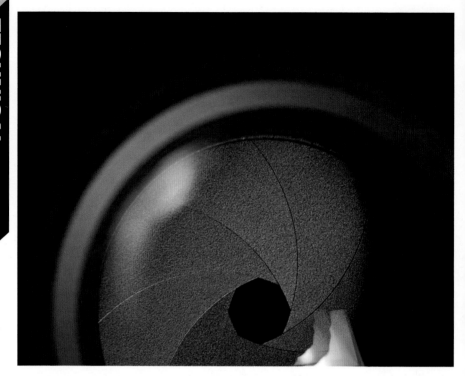

What the shutter does

At the heart of your digital camera lies the sensor. This delicate, sensitive piece of electronic magic is the component that gathers light and transforms it into the data that's eventually stored on your memory card as a JPEG or RAW file.

The shutter mechanism sits in front of the sensor. On a DSLR, this comprises a set of metal or plastic curtains and an angled mirror, which ordinarily directs light up through the camera to the viewfinder. When you press the shutter release, the whole mechanism flies out of the way, the shutter curtains open, and the sensor is activated. Even on a mid-range camera, this whole ballet may happen up to five times a second.

Professional cameras work at up to twice this speed.

How long the shutter is open is known as an exposure, and how long it lasts depends on the effect you're trying to achieve. For instance, if your camera is mounted on a tripod and you want to create a blurring effect, or to capture the light trails on a motorway (see p110), you'll want the shutter to be open for a relatively long time. If, on the other hand, you're taking action shots, you need a very short exposure time to freeze the action crisply.

The length of an exposure also depends on how much light is available. If you're shooting in poor light – at dusk, for instance

Getting a sharp action shot requires a fast shutter speed – in this case, 1/1,000th of a second.

– you'll need the shutter to be open for a long time for the sensor to gather enough light to form an image. Alternatively, if you're taking pictures in bright sunlight, you'll need to keep your shutter speed quick to stop your photo becoming over-exposed.

Shutter speeds are measured in fractions of a second, or whole seconds. For instance, a shutter speed of 1/125th means the sensor will be exposed for 0.008 seconds; that is, a 125th of a second. A shutter speed of 1 means an exposure of one second.

Shutter speeds are described in "stops", and each stop admits twice as much light as the previous one. For instance, a shutter speed of 1/1,000th of a second is one stop faster than 1/500th. A shutter speed of 1/500th is two stops slower than a shutter speed of 1/2,000th of a second. The more you use the manual modes on your camera, the more useful this information becomes – if you take a picture that's heavily over-exposed, you probably need to reduce your exposure by two stops, for instance.

Some lenses, such as this Nikon 85mm f/1.4, offer fantastic low-light performance thanks to their large apertures. The trade-off is weight and price.

What the aperture does

On the previous page we saw how the shutter lies between the lens and the sensor, and affects how long the sensor is exposed. However, it isn't the only way to control the amount of light hitting the sensor. In every lens is an aperture: literally an opening, the size of which can be varied.

The bigger the aperture is set, the more light will hit the sensor at once, and therefore the shorter the exposure you can use. Alternatively, you can reduce the aperture size, which admits less light and allows you to use a longer exposure. Lenses with large maximum apertures are simply known as "fast".

As well as altering the amount of light that comes into the camera, aperture size has a drastic effect on your image's depth of field. If your camera has a small aperture, the image will have a vast depth of field, allowing you to bring both foreground and background objects into focus. If you use a large aperture, your shot will have a narrow depth of field, which means you can focus on only one, very small plane in your image. For example, you might use a large aperture to focus on a small animal, to throw the background out of focus.

Aperture size is measured in f-stops: the smaller the number, the larger the opening relative to the focal length of the lens. Each f-stop number is arrived at by dividing

In this image, a large aperture has allowed plenty of light and the action has been frozen. The potential drawback is that only one tiger can be focused on.

the lens' focal length by the diameter of aperture – so a 100mm lens with an aperture diameter of 25mm is set at f/4, for example. Alternatively, a 500mm lens set at f/4 has an aperture diameter of 125mm. This is why fast telephoto lenses are heavy and expensive: they contain some huge, precisely engineered pieces of glass.

No matter what the focal length of your lens, though, any given f-stop results in the same amount of light hitting the sensor.

So a 500mm lens at f/4 requires the same shutter speed as a 50mm lens set at f/4.

Lighter, cheaper lenses often have variable maximum aperture. The lens that came with your DSLR might have a maximum aperture of f/3.5 when the lens is zoomed out, and f/5.6 when the lens is zoomed in. Constant aperture lenses, which allow you to use the same large aperture no matter how much the lens is zoomed in, are heavier and more expensive.

Modern cameras can produce sensationally clean results at high ISO. This image from a Nikon D3s was taken at ISO 3200.

How to use ISO

ISO is the measure of how sensitive your camera's sensor is at any one time. If you remember the days of film, you'll know that a roll of ISO 200 film was perfect for a day of taking pictures outside, while ISO 800 film was better for indoor photography.

The concept of ISO sensitivity has made the leap to digital photography: the higher the number, the more your camera's sensor will react to any given amount of light. For instance, a low ISO – 200, say – will require a longer shutter time than an ISO of 1600. One of the most significant benefits of digital photography is that changing ISO is as simple as hitting a few buttons; in the days of film, you needed to change the roll.

As with shutter speeds and aperture, ISO can be measured in stops, where each stop results in twice the sensitivity. So ISO 200 is a stop faster than ISO 100, for instance.

It's important to remember that ISO, aperture and shutter speed all work in concert. So if your exposure is fine and you change one setting, you'll need to change something else in the opposite direction for the same exposure. For instance, if you're shooting at 1/800th with an aperture of f/4 and you cut the shutter speed to 1/400th, you'll need to close the aperture a stop (to f/5.6) to get the same amount of light coming in. Alternatively, you could keep the aperture the same and halve the ISO.

The cost of increasing your camera's ISO is noise; this is a random speckling effect that becomes worse the higher the ISO goes. Modern cameras can produce some fantastic results, though. Top-end models from Nikon and Canon can shoot with ISOs of 3200 and higher without an appreciable impact on image quality. Lower-end cameras will generally produce usable results at up to ISO 1600. After that, it's worth assessing whether you can get a good exposure by using a longer shutter speed and a tripod, or by processing your images with noise-reducing software once your files are loaded onto your computer.

It's a different story with consumer compact cameras. This image, taken at ISO 3200, is unusable.

Navigating your camera's controls

On the top of most cameras is a circular control known as the mode dial – this decides how you'll control your camera. You can choose, for instance, to allow your camera to make all its own decisions about metering with the automatic mode (metering is when your camera's internal computer looks at a scene and decides what kind of exposure it needs. This can be based simply on how bright a scene is or, in more complex cases, the kind of scene the camera thinks it's looking at). This mode is generally represented by a green square, and when selected your camera will choose the ISO, exposure and aperture settings itself.

However, your camera can't be relied upon to make great decisions all the time, so you should learn how to use its manual modes. In these modes you take over one or more of the camera's functions, as well as assuming responsibility for setting the ISO. Switching to "A" or "Av", for instance, allows you to set the camera's aperture. It will still choose the shutter speed it thinks is correct.

Alternatively, choosing "S" or "Tv" allows you to choose your own shutter speed, and the camera will select an appropriate aperture value. Finally, the most control – and the most difficulty – is provided by the "M" mode, which hands both shutter and aperture control to you. Capturing good images using this mode requires some experience and practice, but it's the mode with which you'll get the best images from your camera.

A QUICK GUIDE TO THE SYMBOLS ON YOUR CAMERA

WB: allows you to quickly choose from a menu of white balance presets, or use a reference (such as a white sheet of paper) if you're in unusual lighting.

ISO: brings up a screen from which you can quickly choose an ISO setting. Not all cameras have a dedicated button for this, but it's handy.

METERING: determines the kind of metering your camera does. Options include evaluative, which looks at the entire scene and determines the exposure required; centre-weighted, which gives priority to a patch in the middle; and spot, which looks only at a small dot, normally in the middle of the viewfinder, to determine exposure.

AF: allows you to choose which autofocus mode your camera should use. Options include single shot, in which the lens attempts to focus when you half-press the shutter button, and continuous, or AI Servo, which attempts to track a subject as it moves away or nearer to you. Most DSLRs also allow you to choose individual autofocus points.

DRIVE: this decides what happens when you keep your finger down on the shutter-release button. In single-shot mode, nothing happens. In continuous mode, your camera will continue firing shots as fast as it can until its built-in memory buffer (not to be confused with the memory card you store images on) is full.

Most cameras have a built-in flash – but it's best to save it for emergencies only.

Notes on flash

Unless you own a particularly high-end camera, your DSLR is likely to have come with an integrated flash. It might be fully automatic – meaning it pops up on its own when your camera decides there isn't enough light – or it might be semi-automatic, which means you need to push a button to pop up the flash and activate it.

You shouldn't write off your integrated flash. In a situation where you don't have a tripod and can't find a shutter speed that results in a blur-free shot, it's a good backup. However, your photographic

wish-list should definitely include a standalone flashgun at some point, because it can make a huge difference.

A flashgun slots into the hotshoe on the top of your camera, assuming it has one; most compact cameras don't, but most DSLRs do. The flashgun normally varies its brightness and focal length depending on what your camera tells it to do, and there are various advantages to using one.

First, a flashgun will be far more powerful than the integrated flash in your camera, allowing it to throw more light over more of

Off-camera flashes, such as this high-end unit from Canon, have the potential to make a huge difference to your photography.

the frame at once – this would be vital if you're at a gig, for instance.

Second, the integrated flash on your camera will always point straight ahead; the best fail-safe option, but it means your subjects will invariably be blinded when it goes off. Such a flash also creates harsh, unnatural-looking shadows. A hotshoe flash, by contrast, can be adjusted. You can point it straight up, say, or off to one side, allowing you to bounce the light off a nearby wall. This light will be softer and more flattering

for your subject, making it look as if they were being lit by natural light.

Finally, a hotshoe flash can be mounted off the camera entirely. You can connect it with a cable or even use a wireless system to set it off when the camera's shutter opens. This gives you the ultimate in flexibility, allowing you to light your subject from wherever you like, as well as giving you the option to use multiple flashes from multiple angles – great for studio photography.

Choosing memory cards

One of the first purchases most photographers make is a new memory card. While the obvious advantage is more storage, choosing the right card can also improve your camera's performance.

There are many different formats of memory card used by cameras, from CompactFlash to Memory Stick Pro, microSD to xD Picture cards. However, the dominant type is the SD card, and fortunately it's easy to find out what type of memory card your camera takes – just open up the slot and take a look.

Before you buy a new card, however, make sure it's going to be fast enough. A card that's too slow could hold you back when shooting multiple RAW files or in burst mode – once the buffer is full, you're reliant on your card's speed.

Take a close look at the specifications. Some manufacturers quote "x" ratings that sound better than they are: for example, 26x equates to only 4MB/sec. Also, the MB/sec rating you see quoted may be a read speed: the rate at which you can transfer the card's contents to your computer. While high

read speeds are beneficial – especially if you have a large amount of data to transfer – they don't reveal how quickly a card performs in-camera.

That's why, if in-camera performance is your priority, you should focus on write speeds: the higher you choose, the less the card will slow you down if it needs to transfer a batch of RAW files from the buffer, or a massive HD video.

You may see the word "Class" when choosing an SD card. This is a measurement of the guaranteed *continuous* write speed, which is most relevant when recording video. Class 2 or Class 4 cards can write at continuous speeds of 2MB/sec and 4MB/sec respectively, which may not be enough for your camera. We'd lean towards either Class 6 or Class 10 – that is, a card capable of writing continuously with rates of at least 6MB/sec or 10MB/sec.

As a shortcut for performance, if you're buying an SD card, look out for SDXC as opposed to SDHC. The HC stands for High Capacity, since this standard extended the maximum storage from the 2GB of the

As this snapshot of SanDisk's range of memory cards shows, there's a wide choice of capacities, formats and speeds to choose from.

first SD cards to 32GB. Now, SDXC (eXtended Capacity) cards go from 64GB to a theoretical 2TB in size. However, their other big benefit is that they typically offer faster write and read speeds.

Storage capacity also needs to be considered. If your 10-megapixel camera is shooting in RAW then you'll only be able to store around 50 shots per gigabyte. A 16-megapixel camera has space for only 40 per gigabyte. Choose the largest card you can afford; the sweet spot is typically one or two steps below the largest current card available.

Finally, be wary when buying memory cards from unofficial sources. While we wouldn't go so far as to avoid eBay – it sometimes offers good value – it's open to abuse. Look out for no-name cards, and if a seller claims to be offering well-known brands then double-check their customer ratings before you buy.

PORTRAITS

Most photographers end up with a category of photography they enjoy more than any other. However, whatever that ends up being for you, you'll probably still take more pictures of people than any other subject. As "the one with the camera", you'll become the de facto photographer at family gatherings, on holiday and during weekends away.

However, as your family's photographer, you'll need to pick up a few tricks to keep things moving; no-one wants to stand with a rictus smile on their face while you battle with shutter and aperture settings, and there are few things more effective at killing the mood at parties than an overly keen photographer getting in the way.

This chapter will help you understand how to get the best photographs of people from any situation, in a variety of light. It also covers tricky situations such as photographing children (good luck). Plus, we reveal the kit you might need to take your social photography from good to great.

020 In the bag
022 Group portraits
024 Perfect photos of children
026 Taking shots of individuals
030 Enhanced lighting

IN THE BAG

Portrait photography is similar to landscape photography in terms of the demands it places on your kit. If you have a DSLR with a reasonable 18-55mm kit lens, you're off to a good start. If your kit lens is stabilised, so much the better, as you'll be able to shoot handheld in worse light.

A very wide-angle lens is outright undesirable for portrait photography. Even the best wide-angle optics distort, making people's foreheads look much larger than they actually are – not an effect your subjects will thank you for.

1 TELEPHOTO LENS

A telephoto lens, on the other hand, can be useful. If you want to shoot frame-filling portraits, then something in the region of 100mm will allow you to take flattering portraits without needing to get so close to people that their breath fogs up the lens.

2 FAST LENS

You'll manage some spectacular results if you use a fast lens. A lens with a maximum aperture of f/2.8 or larger will allow you to achieve spectacular depth-of-field effects, isolating your subject from their background and emphasising their face.

3 FLASHGUN

Decent light is essential for portrait photography. This can simply mean using natural light and paying attention to how

bright it is and where it's coming from, or taking advantage of household spotlights. Alternatively, an external flashgun is a good investment – a decent one will likely outlast your current camera, and higher-end models have advanced manual modes. A manual mode won't be much use at first, but the more you shoot, the more you'll want the extra features. An off-camera flash cable is also useful: it costs around £20, and allows flexibility in terms of precisely what angle the light is coming from. A reflector is another potentially desirable tool, too.

4 TRIPOD

A tripod isn't strictly necessary. When you're taking pictures of people, the ability to move around freely, without dragging a support with you, is helpful. However, the more complicated your light setup, the more likely you are to want your camera to remain in precisely the same place. Also, if you're using your flash off-camera, being able to support your light on a tripod is a better solution than attempting to aim your flash with one hand and your camera with the other.

1

2

3

4

Group

PORTRAITS

Group portraits are tricky. Not only are there technical considerations, but you're also going to have to work fast – all it takes is for one person to get bored and wander off and your shot is ruined. You can roughly halve the available time if your group includes children. Follow these tips to get great results every time.

Static groups of people simply look like they're milling around: getting a gathering to do something interesting is both fun and will result in better shots.

1 BE CREATIVE

Assembling your group into a haphazard mass and expecting interesting shots to result is a fool's errand. In the carefully timed shot above, the group was instructed to jump just before the camera fired. As a result, the final image not only has plenty of energy, but the group looks happy and engaged, which makes for a better image.

2 KEEP IT FAST

A fast shutter speed was used here to freeze the motion of the jumpers, but a decent shutter speed of 1/250th or faster is a good baseline for a group of people. Nothing sucks the fun out of an afternoon like barking at a group to keep perfectly still: using a fast shutter speed will ensure they don't have to.

3 USE LIGHT CAREFULLY

Even though this shot was taken outside, the group has been illuminated from both sides with powerful professional flashguns. This extra light not only means a faster shutter speed, but it also adds contrast and glamour to the resulting shot. Flashguns aren't just for indoors and low light!

Perfect photos of
CHILDREN

As every parent knows, most children love nothing more than sitting absolutely still while a photographer sorts out his or her camera kit. But if, for some strange reason, you meet a child that doesn't conform, you'll need a few tricks in your arsenal to capture a decent picture.

1 ACT NATURAL

Trying to get a child to pose will make them feel self-conscious and withdrawn. Conversely, a child at ease will ignore you, allowing you to get on with taking pictures. Treat taking photographs of children as you would if you were a photojournalist covering a breaking news story. Shoot without getting in the way.

2 SHOOT A LOT

The shot on the right was relatively pre-meditated, but children will present you with lots of photographic opportunities, and taking a lot of pictures will allow you to choose the very best. Also, as kids move around a lot (often quite fast) your camera's autofocus is going to struggle occasionally. Shooting plenty of frames will increase your chances of a sharp shot.

3 ADD PROPS

Kids love to play, and a few props or a well-stocked toy box will give you far more interesting scenes to capture. Photographically, remember that bold colours always work well, and that children like nothing more than dressing up. Hats and sunglasses are the order of the day.

■ AT-A-GLANCE SETTINGS

SHUTTER SPEED	1/60TH
APERTURE	F/5.6
ISO	200
FOCAL LENGTH	59mm
FLASH	EXTERNAL

Props are always winners when photographing kids, as they serve the dual functions of distracting your subject from the process, and being interesting to look at.

Photographing

INDIVIDUALS

Photographing people in public requires a mixture of technical skill and the ability to beguile total strangers into posing. Nailing the technical side will let you make the most of your opportunities.

Doing justice to a person in a single photo is a tall order. In a fraction of a second, you're hoping to produce something that will resonate with others even if they don't know the person in the picture. And you have to be quick: at some point between asking someone if you can take their picture and firing the shutter, you must nail down the exposure you want, your ISO setting, set your focal length, and compose a shot that won't need correcting later.

1 COMPOSE CAREFULLY
Imagine a set of four evenly spaced gridlines on your viewfinder. Two lines run horizontally, two vertically. By placing key objects in your photos at the intersections of these lines, you can guide people's eyes and keep them interested in your photos. In this photo, the man's head is perfectly placed two-thirds of the way up the photo, and two-thirds towards the right. This strong composition makes up for the lack of eye contact. His gaze – diagonally down across the frame – guides our eye towards the puppy.

2 CHOOSE YOUR FOCAL LENGTH
A wide-angle lens is poor for portraiture, as it distorts. In this instance, knowledge of the lens at hand meant it was pre-set to a distortion-free setting of 35mm, and the composition was achieved through the time-honoured method of moving forwards until the frame was filled. Trying to adjust composition by turning your lens' zoom ring isn't the best way to compose a shot!

3 CHOOSE YOUR DEPTH OF FIELD CAREFULLY
This shot was taken in a busy Chinese market; fiddling with camera dials and stressing over aperture settings would have meant missed shots. Shooting at ISO 100, an aperture of f/8 produced a shutter speed of 1/50th. f/8 has ensured the right balance between sharpness for our two subjects, while pushing the background wall slightly out of focus to make the man and his dog stand out. If the light isn't changing, you can set your camera to a particular exposure and leave it there.

▊ AT-A-GLANCE SETTINGS

SHUTTER SPEED	1/50TH
APERTURE	F/8
ISO	100
FOCAL LENGTH	35MM
EXPOSURE	TV

A mid-range aperture has resulted in a shot in which the crucial elements are sharp, while the background is diffused.

BREAKING THE RULES

This image doesn't follow any of the rules of portrait photography, but it's still engaging. It doesn't follow the rule of thirds: the subject's mouth is a third of the way up the frame, but her eyes are halfway up. Eye contact is missing, too; generally considered important in portrait photography, eye contact is great to have as it instantly hooks viewers in. However, this image has features that help its rule-breaking to work. For instance, what it lacks in eye contact it gains in framing and composition. The hat frames our subject's face, drawing the eye in. The subject also totally fills the frame. The use of a large aperture means the front of the hat and the blue scarf at lower right are out of focus, drawing the eye in when traditional hooks aren't available.

▌ AT-A-GLANCE SETTINGS

SHUTTER SPEED	1/125TH
APERTURE	F/5
ISO	1000
FOCAL LENGTH	41MM

2008
1984
1992
2000
2032

SANDISK TESTED
UP TO
100
YEARS
ESTIMATED STORAGE LIFE

The NEW   SanDisk® Memory Vault

Will your memories still be there
in 10 years... 20... 30...?

Hard drives have moving parts. DVDs may scratch. Photos may fade over time.
So don't let your digital memories become distant memories. The new SanDisk
Memory Vault storage device uses unique memory technology to ensure
preservation of your photos and videos for up to 100 years.

Now you can preserve your precious digital
photos and videos for future generations

SanDisk®

1972   1978   1986   1990   1992   1995   1999   2001   2003   2

Enhanced
LIGHTING

A photographer's job is working with light, and an appreciation of how to use what's available will make a huge difference. However, there will be times when natural light isn't enough, and it's in these situations that an external flash will come into its own.

Your camera probably has a flash built in: pop a bit of tape over it and never use it again. A dedicated flash that mounts in your camera's hotshoe – the metal bracket directly above the viewfinder – is by far the best option. You'll be able to adjust the direction of the flash, which means you can bounce light off a ceiling or a wall, instead of popping the flash straight into your subject's eyes. You'll also be able to adjust the power of your flash and, with a remote cable, fire your flash even when it isn't attached to the camera.

1 USE FILL-IN FLASH

When you use a flash, you don't need to think of it as replacing light that's already available. Instead, in the shot on the right, there's already lots of light coming from the sun, but it's facing almost directly into the camera. Firing a low-powered flash allowed a faster shutter speed, while preserving detail in the background and ensuring plenty of detail on the subject's face. The photogenic lens-flare is a plus.

2 USE A REFLECTOR

Another option with this kind of shot is to place a silver or gold reflector at the subject's feet. Expect to pay in the region of £10-£20 for one. In this case, we could have capitalised on the bright sun by placing a reflector in front of our subject and not using a flash at all. Positioning a reflector does mean a more involved and protracted setup, though, as well as normally requiring an assistant to hold it.

3 USE FLASH COMPENSATION

If your flash doesn't have a fully manual mode, you should be able to use flash compensation to change how powerfully your flash fires. If you find that your flash is blinding people, or you want to carefully adjust the contrast between the background and foreground of your image, turning your flash down will help. Alternatively, if you're shooting somewhere very dark, or you want a harsh, bright image, you can turn up your flash compensation for a brighter pop.

▋ AT-A-GLANCE SETTINGS

SHUTTER SPEED   1/200TH
APERTURE   F/10
ISO   100
FOCAL LENGTH   28MM
FLASH   EXTERNAL

Backlit subjects often require fill-in flash to make sure their faces aren't obscured in shadow. An off-camera flash gives you added flexibility.

LANDSCAPES

3

LANDSCAPES

If portrait photography is about telling the story of a person, then landscape photography is all about telling the story of a place. Although the name conjures up rustic scenes, a landscape photograph can be a picture of virtually anywhere.

Look up landscape photography on the internet and you'll find a host of highfalutin rules, most of which you can safely disregard – notions such as lead-in lines and the rule of thirds are nothing more than good starting points for a great photo. It's arguably more important to have an appreciation of light, backed up by the technique tips in this chapter to help you achieve technically solid shots. This will allow you to concentrate on producing great images of your favourite places.

Besides an appreciation for nature, there are a few pieces of equipment that will help capture the perfect image. Aside from that, your best friend is likely to be an appreciation of the world in front of you – and it takes a lot of appreciation to drive a person from their bed before it even gets light.

3

034 In the bag
036 Shooting at dawn
038 Using unusual frame sizes
040 Using graduated filters
042 Using a tilt-shift lens
044 Maximising depth of field and sharpness

IN THE BAG

Landscape photography is a great place to start since it doesn't require much specialised kit. If you have a DSLR and a kit lens, you already have enough to take fantastic pictures – you don't need a particularly fast lens or incredible ISO performance to take a decent shot. Most DSLR kit lenses run from wide-angle to mid-range zoom, which is all the focal length required to get a good shot. Just find some appealing countryside and snap away!

As with all photographic disciplines, though, you'll quickly discover that you can add new styles and techniques by using different pieces of kit. Although you don't necessarily need any of it to capture a good shot, using the right gear can help your photos stand out from the crowd.

1 GRADUATED FILTER

The sky is often a lot brighter than land, creating problems as you can expose only for one or the other. A graduated filter is dark at the top and clear at the bottom, allowing you to properly expose land at the bottom of the frame, and still have plenty of detail in the sky at the top. See p40 for more on graduated filters.

2 TILT-SHIFT LENS

These specialist lenses are often reserved for architectural photography. But being able to correct perspective and focus on any plane in your image has plenty of applications for landscapes. See p42.

3 HEAD LAMP

As with any outdoor photography, the best vantage points are often worth arriving at before it's light, or leaving after the sun has set. A decent head lamp will allow you to transport your expensive camera kit without tumbling down the side of a mountain.

4 TRIPOD

If shooting landscapes with long exposure times, you'll need something to rest your camera on while the shutter is open. A stabilised lens will work only to a maximum of around half a second without blurring. Buy a tripod that's lightweight and folds up.

5 ULTRA-WIDE LENS

If you're taking pictures of grand scenery such as vast mountain ranges, a lens that can take pictures at a focal length of around 10mm will allow you to take in the whole expanse at once. Beware using an ultra-wide lens on less majestic scenes, as you risk making the scenery look insignificant.

6 ND FILTER

Photographs of water – the tide coming in, for instance – can look sterile if you've frozen the moment with a short exposure. An ND filter allows you to use slow shutter speeds by darkening the lens and drastically reducing the amount of incoming light.

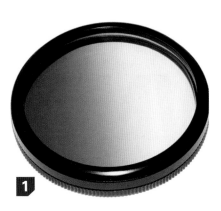

1

3

CANON LENS TS-E 24mm 1:3.5 II

Canon
TS-E 24mm

2

4

Nikon
AF-S NIKKOR 10-24mm 1:3.5-4.5G ED
DX

5

3

58mm   PL-CIR   JAPAN

6

Shooting at

DAWN

Photography is all about making the most of light. If you head out to take landscape photographs in the middle of the day, you'll end up with rather flat shots. The sun is directly overhead and at its very brightest – which means harsh, direct lighting.

Visit a local beauty spot just before dawn, however, and you'll be treated to the "golden hour", so-called by photographers because the sunlight has a warm, orange hue. Light also hits the scenery at an angle, creating interesting shadows. Not only that, but you'll also find that few other photographers have the foresight (or resolve) to set their alarm clocks, all-but guaranteeing you a front-row seat at even the most popular beauty spots.

1 PLAN AHEAD
Since you'll be arriving at your landscape pre-dawn – or leaving it after sunset – it's worth scoping it out ahead of time. That way you'll know if the nearest car park is open, how long it takes to hike to the best vantage point, and if there are any open wells to fall down on the way there.

2 USE A SMALL APERTURE
If you use a large aperture (f/5.6 or smaller) you'll be able to use a quick shutter speed, which means sharp shots, even handheld. However, at this setting you'll find that you can't focus on much of your scene at once. Use a longer shutter speed and smaller aperture – f/11 or f/16 are ideal for landscapes.

3 STABILISE
Since you're using a small aperture, you should find that your camera wants to use exposure times of upwards of one second. It's impossible to take a steady shot handheld at this speed, so use a tripod, or rest your camera on something level. If you can, use a remote control to fire the shutter, so the action of you taking your hand off the camera doesn't blur the image. If you don't have a remote, set your camera's self-timer to two seconds and use that instead.

To achieve the best possible landscape, shoot at dawn or sunset to make the most of the sun's warm hues.

■ AT-A-GLANCE SETTINGS

SHUTTER SPEED	1/250TH
APERTURE	F/5.6
ISO	100
FOCAL LENGTH	17MM
EXPOSURE	+/-0

■ **AT-A-GLANCE SETTINGS**

SHUTTER SPEED	1/1,600TH
APERTURE	F/4
ISO	100
FOCAL LENGTH	22MM
PHOTO-EDITING SOFTWARE TO CROP	

Using unusual

FRAME SIZES

Not all landscape photography requires an ultra-wide-angle lens. While such lenses are ideal for shots of grand mountain ranges, on occasion, the standard 18-55mm kit lens supplied with most mainstream DSLRs will suffice.

Even if you use that standard lens, you'll find images that don't require the whole frame. Help is at hand, however. Modern cameras provide huge amounts of resolution, and

that means in many cases you can crop into your images, removing unnecessary parts of the frame. This is helpful in landscape photography: cropping your shot so it's

Cropping your
landscape shot so
it's very wide and
short will give
you an instant
panorama!

very wide and short can make a vista look much wider, without needing to go to the considerable hassle of manually stitching photos together to create a panorama.

1 RESOLVE, RESOLVE, RESOLVE

If you aren't already using the best quality setting on your camera, switch to it now. Cropping to a more appropriate frame size requires you to ditch large areas of your shot and may enlarge areas that may go unseen. If there's obvious compression or lots of noise in your shot, this will make the most of it. For the same reason, make sure any landscape shot that might be a candidate for cropping is perfectly focused.

2 THINK PRINT

You'll need to use a photo editor to crop your shot, but don't rush in. Eventually you'll want to print the image, and that's going to

be difficult if you've used a never-seen-before size. Check which panoramic sizes your printer uses, and resize to one of them. In an editor such as Photoshop Elements, you can enter the final dimensions of your image in centimetres or inches once you've selected the Crop tool.

3 THINK IN MULTIPLES

Triptychs are effective ways of using cropped work. If you can find three images that work well together when cropped to the same size – an image of the sea, a mountain range and a desert, for instance – cropping them and using them in the same frame or on the same wall could look amazing.

Using graduated

FILTERS

Balancing exposure between sky and earth is a juggling act. Using a graduated filter, either physical or in software, is a simple way to get the picture you want.

On a perfect day, with blue skies, it's possible to take technically great pictures every time. However, even with the best weather, you're likely to find your landscape photographs have either over-exposed clouds, or severely under-exposed land. The reason? The contrast between the light clouds and the dark earth is so great that your camera can expose for only one or the other.

The answer is to use a graduated filter: a thin strip of glass that sits in front of your camera's lens. It starts dark at the top, and fades to totally transparent. The result? Less light from the top half of your image (the clouds) reaches your camera's sensor, so the clouds look darker when the image is finished.

Using a filter is relatively simple. With the filter removed, set your camera so you get a good exposure of the ground in the frame. Manual mode is best for this – otherwise, your camera's

settings may change when you attach the filter or recompose. Once you have an image you're happy with, pop in the filter and shoot at the same settings. The ground will be exposed the same, but the sky will be significantly darker.

If using a filter is simple, choosing one is more difficult. How much under-exposure you'll need at the top depends on how dark the clouds are, so different weather calls for different filters – not ideal when a graduated filter is likely to cost from £50.

However, once you've grasped the concept of essentially needing two different exposures for the ground and sky, the effect is simple to reproduce in software. As with a physical filter, expose for the ground and allow the sky to over-expose slightly. When you're back, you can use software to correct the top half of your photo. How complex this task is varies between applications, but it's a useful technique to be able to perform.

■ AT-A-GLANCE SETTINGS

SHUTTER SPEED	1/400TH
APERTURE	F/8
ISO	200
FOCAL LENGTH	26MM

Photo-editing software has added the effect of a graduated filter to the sky.

Using a tilt-shift

LENS

Forget your step-ladder? A tilt-shift lens allows you to dramatically shift your apparent eye-point without moving your feet. Alternatively, you can use it to tilt the focal plane relative to your camera's sensor and create a totally new perspective.

Whatever you're photographing, it's important to find the best possible vantage point. Normally, this is simple – just move around your subject until you find the best angle. Even with landscape photography, getting higher or lower is almost always possible. There will always be an exception, though, where taking a picture of something that's taller than you requires you to crane your neck upwards. This isn't always great for photography: the picture of the church steeple on p30 works because all the other buildings in the picture are level, giving the impression that we're looking straight at it across the rooftops. However, to obtain the elevated eye level required for the image, a tilt-shift lens was used.

1 SHIFTING
The "shift" part of a tilt-shift lens' name comes from the fact that you can move the viewpoint of the lens away from the centre line of the camera. So if you want to shoot up at something, you can shift the viewpoint up without needing to tilt the camera. Alternatively, you could shoot sideways without needing to turn your body.

2 TILTING
Tilting is an entirely different story. Your camera's focal plane is normally perpendicular to the sensor, so things the same distance from the sensor will be focused. By tilting the lens relative to the sensor, as in the image on the right, the focal plane lies at an angle to the sensor, allowing you to focus on a narrow plane no matter how far the objects on the plane are from the camera and each other.

3 MANUAL MODE
Your camera's automatic metering is useless with a tilt-shift lens once you start using either its tilt or shift functions. To get around this, use your camera's manual mode to get your exposure right before you shoot.

AT-A-GLANCE SETTINGS

SHUTTER SPEED   1/1,250TH
APERTURE   F/2.8
ISO   400
FOCAL LENGTH   45MM
TILT-SHIFT LENS

■ AT-A-GLANCE SETTINGS

SHUTTER SPEED	1/125TH
APERTURE	F/16
ISO	320
FOCAL LENGTH	45mm
EXPOSURE	MANUAL

Maximising depth of field and

SHARPNESS

Depth of field is useful for some subjects, but you don't need it for landscapes. Here's how to adjust your camera's settings to produce the sharpest possible results.

A vast landscape such as this needs to be sharp from the front of the frame to the back to retain people's interest.

Most of the time, your camera's ability to produce images with good depth of field is useful. For instance, if you're taking a picture of a person, being able to blur the background and bring their face into focus is a good way of highlighting the subject. Similarly, with still-life images, being able to be selective in terms of what's in focus is a useful creative trick.

This is rarely the case with landscape photography. Particularly with grand views, the eye wants to explore the entire image, from the top of the mountain you're standing on to the tiny hills and towns in the distance. If your image isn't

sharp from the front to the back, people's eyes will be prevented from seeing every detail in a scene, which can feel frustrating. Maintaining sharpness takes care and attention more than anything else – here's how to avoid the blurs.

1 APERTURE

Use a small aperture. Big apertures are useful for letting in lots of light, but you get shallow depth of field. A small aperture lets in less light, which means a longer exposure, but it also means better depth of field. As long as one part of your image is in focus, the rest will look as if it is too. If you have good weather – or a tripod – set your camera to aperture priority mode and use f/16. If you're shooting handheld in overcast weather, f/11 is a reasonable substitute. Avoid anything lower than f/8.

2 SHUTTER SPEED

As discussed in the wildlife section (see chapter 4), a good rule of thumb with shutter speeds is to use one over the focal length to avoid camera shake. So, if you're using a 45mm lens, set your shutter speed to 1/50th of a second or faster. A stabilised lens will allow you to use a slower speed still.

3 IMAGE BLUR

If you're using a tripod, use a remote control to fire the shutter, so the action of taking your hand off the camera doesn't blur the image. If you don't have a remote, set your camera's self-timer to two seconds and use that instead.

WILDLIFE

Wildlife photography is one of the most challenging forms of photography. Unpredictable light, combined with distant, nervous subjects, means a decent sighting can be difficult, much less turning that glimpse into a sharp photo.

Having the right kit with you can help (see p48), as moving close to some animals is either impossible or dangerous, so a long lens will make all the difference. Similarly, you'll find some fast-moving birds might require a camera capable of capturing multiple frames per second (see p56). You'll also need to get to grips with using your camera's autofocus mode (see p60) – wildlife photography is one area that doesn't reward popping your camera on fully automatic mode and hoping for the best. Even zoo photography has its quirks, which you'll need to work out if you want to bring home perfect images (see p52).

For photography in the wild you'll need to up your game further. Wild animal photography takes careful planning, tremendous patience, and no small amount of luck. The trick is to make sure that when a once-in-a-lifetime event happens within range of your camera, you have the skills to capture it.

048 In the bag
050 Wildlife from afar
052 Getting good shots at the zoo
056 Shooting garden birds
058 Capturing movement
060 Using autofocus

IN THE BAG

Don't be put off – just because professional photographers (of all stripes, not just wildlife) use heavy and expensive equipment, doesn't mean you have to. Decent-quality telephoto lenses and fast bodies can be bought for surprisingly little, and don't forget that sites such as eBay or reputable camera dealers are often great places to look for used, high-performance bodies and lenses.

2 ULTRA-TELEPHOTO LENS

If, on the other hand, you want to capture full-frame images of small garden birds, or small, nervous mammals such as otters, you'll need more reach. For more ambitious wildlife photography a lens that reaches to 400mm is exceedingly useful. However, you'll need fast shutter speeds to achieve steady exposures at this focal length, and that means lenses with large apertures – it's this that pushes the cost of ultra-fast, ultra-long telephoto lenses into the thousands of pounds, along with their lightning-fast autofocus speed.

1 STANDARD TELEPHOTO LENS

How long a lens you use depends on what you're shooting. If you're taking pictures of large, relatively tame animals – such as horses, deer or elephants – you don't need a massive lens. A standard 70-300mm will do, and you can get these for less than £300. Cheaper lenses such as these will be relatively slow in terms of their maximum aperture – you'll probably be looking at a maximum of f/5.6 when zoomed all the way in, which needs either very good light or a high ISO speed.

3 PHOTOGRAPHER'S BACKPACK

Photographers are spoilt for choice when it comes to bags, with specialist manufacturers such as Lowepro offering everything from rucksacks to shoulder bags to hard cases – and much more besides. A tech-loving photographer, one who likes to carry round their laptop and tablet (which can make an amazing remote viewfinder), should consider the Booq Python backpack. It isn't cheap – costing more than £200 – but it's built to supreme levels of quality, has a water-repellent outer shell, and includes space for laptops up to 15in in size while squeezing in mini-compartments for up to four lenses.

4 RAIN JACKET FOR CAMERA

Anyone who's set off for a day trip in the UK will know that although it may start off sunny, it can end up like a tropical storm – so it isn't only you who needs protection from the elements. A rain jacket is the best bet, especially if it's specifically designed for your DSLR: you'll be able to gain quick access to all the essential controls. While these can be expensive, you can also buy simple rainsleeves for as little as £6.

5 SOME SUPPORT

There's a fair amount of waiting involved with wildlife photography, and while most camera and lens combinations can be comfortably hefted up to shoot, if you have to hold the position for more than a minute you might find yourself with backache the following day. A decent monopod is portable, packs up neatly, and will take the strain off your arms.

Wildlife from

[AFAR]

Most wild animals aren't keen on humans being too close, so to grab a good shot you'll often need to rely on long lenses. Like any piece of photo gear, these take a bit of getting used to before you'll be able to shoot effectively – but the results will be worth it.

1 USE AN APPROPRIATE SHUTTER SPEED

Here's a general rule: the slowest shutter speed you should use on your camera is one over the focal length of your lens. So, if you're using a 400mm lens, the slowest shutter speed you can use handheld is 1/400th. This doesn't take into account factors such as use of a tripod, how steady your hands are, or whether your lens has image stabilisation built in – but it's a good place to start. Wildlife moves around a lot, so to take a good portrait you need to use the fastest shutter speed you can. If you want to catch animals in motion – such as birds in flight – you should start with at least 1/1,000th of a second, possibly faster.

2 USE A LARGE APERTURE

A large aperture gives you lots of light to work with, which in turn means a faster shutter speed. It will also give you a narrower depth of field, which will help isolate your subject from its background. If using a large aperture and a quick shutter speed still doesn't give you the exposure you want, raise the ISO before sacrificing crispness by lowering the exposure time.

3 DON'T STOP MOVING YOUR FEET

A long lens is heavy and tricky to manoeuvre, but don't let that stop you constantly moving to get the best vantage point. Owners of versatile long-range zoom lenses will often be tempted to stay in one point and simply "zoom in" on their subjects – but you'll get the best shots if you set your focal length first and move around to compose your shot.

4 STAY STEADY

The bigger the lens, the more difficult it is to hold it in position while you wait for an animal to enter the frame. That's fine with lightweight budget zooms, but for more substantial bits of kit you'll either need very strong arms, or a monopod that can take the weight, allowing you to concentrate on looking for wildlife. Having your camera constantly raised and ready will reduce your reaction times as well.

Tigers aren't noted for their approachability, so a long lens is a must for frame-filling portraits. In this case, a long focal length of 400mm was used, along with a large aperture of 5.6 to isolate the animal from the background.

▮ AT-A-GLANCE SETTINGS

SHUTTER SPEED	1/160TH
APERTURE	F/5.6
ISO	1250
FOCAL LENGTH	400MM
EXPOSURE	AV

Good shots at the

ZOO

Zoos offer amazing photo opportunities and are great for practice – but be honest about where your shots are from!

Your local zoo or wildlife park is the perfect place to start experimenting with wildlife photography. The animals you'll see will be habituated to people, and are well-placed for the best visibility. The practice is invaluable – but with zoos so popular, and decent cameras so accessible, you'll find your vantage point is shared by plenty of other would-be photographers. Here's how to bring home shots that are a cut above the rest.

1 GET THE EYES RIGHT

A mantra for wildlife photographers is the need to "get the eyes right". An animal with sharply focused eyes will look personable, and gives the viewer's eye an immediate point of contact with the image. There are lots of opportunities to break this rule depending on the effect you want to achieve – but it's a good place to start.

2 KEEP IT QUICK

The otter on the right doesn't appear to be moving, but the fact is animals hold still for about the same length of time as kids. This means using a fast shutter speed; we shot the above at 1/1,250th of a second. The flipside of that is a large aperture. We set f/5.6 to get plenty of light to the sensor, at the cost of foreground sharpness.

■ AT-A-GLANCE SETTINGS

SHUTTER SPEED	1/1,250TH
APERTURE	F/5.6
ISO	1000
FOCAL LENGTH	300MM
EXPOSURE	MANUAL

3 FORGET THE MONSTER LENS

No zoo on the planet requires you to bring a massive telescope of a lens. The animals simply aren't that far away, and all you'll do is annoy other visitors who trip over your kit. Instead, stick to something practical and restrained: a 70-200mm lens is enough, and a 70-300mm lens more than generous. Leave the flash at home.

4 LUNCHTIME!

Most zoos and wildlife parks have feeding times. Animals will come out when food appears, and photogenically squabble for the choicest bites. More intelligent animals will learn when they're going to be fed, and will be active in their enclosures before feeding time. Pick up a day planner when you arrive and use it!

SHOOTING THROUGH FENCES

You can't tell, but the picture above was shot through a chain-link fence. But, instead of spending laborious hours editing the photo to remove the fence, we used a much simpler technique. If you use a decent focal length and a large aperture, your camera has a very shallow depth of field, which means only a small slice of the frame will be focused. Push your lens up against the fence and focus on something a reasonable distance away, and the fence will dissolve. Your image may darken slightly because of the reduced light hitting the sensor, but you should be presented with a crisp, fence-free image.

■ AT-A-GLANCE SETTINGS

SHUTTER SPEED	1/1,000TH
APERTURE	F/5.6
ISO	1000
FOCAL LENGTH	400MM
EXPOSURE	MANUAL

ADVENTURE

UNCOMPROMISING PHOTOGRAPHY BY DAVID NEWTON

"Having spent over 3 hours watching the lion eat his fill and shooting 20 GB of pictures, I became aware of how glad I was to have large capacity cards. The last thing I wanted to do was risk having to change cards mid-way through the action and miss something spectacular."

"You'll be surprised how quickly the shots run out when the action starts, so it's risky having just 30 or 40 shots left on your card. And, whether it's lions on the African plains or wildlife closer to home, I find shooting burst mode on super-fast SanDisk Extreme Pro® memory cards a great advantage even for relatively static subjects."

David Newton is a member of the SanDisk Extreme® Team, a select group of professional photographers whose vision is as uncompromising as their equipment.

 See us on Facebook for the full story, tips, videos and portfolios:
www.facebook.com/sandiskextremeteam

Shooting

GARDEN BIRDS

Whether you live in the middle of a city or the middle of nowhere, it's more than likely any outdoor space to which you have access – a garden, a balcony or simply a window ledge – can play host to an astonishing array of wildlife. With a bit of planning, you can take some cracking photographs without even having to leave the comfort of your house.

1 THINK BIG

Garden birds are small. In fact, some of the UK's iconic species such as robins or blue tits will fit in the palm of your hand. Shooting a full-frame portrait will require you to be either very close, or be using a long lens; 300mm is a minimum, with 400mm preferable and, if you can afford it, 500mm perfect. The picture on the right was taken with a 400mm lens, and then cropped.

2 SSSHHHH

Some garden birds are gregarious little fellows that will allow you to move surprisingly close before darting off the branch. Others will vanish if you twitch your little finger. Two things will help you obtain better shots. The first is to stock up on bird food and start leaving it out; birds will quickly learn that your garden is a safe bet for their morning feed. The second is to shoot from a hide, allowing you to be close without scaring the birds.

3 BEWARE BACKGROUNDS

Photographing birds in trees will always present you with problems, since the background is likely to be cluttered with other branches, which means the viewer's eye will be snatched all over the place. Using a large aperture (f/4 or larger) will help diffuse the background and rob it of detail, but your best bet is to be selective about where you leave bird food: leave it on a branch with a background you know works visually. Alternatively, waiting for birds that eat worms to land on the ground can help solve the problem.

▌AT-A-GLANCE SETTINGS

SHUTTER SPEED	1/400TH
APERTURE	F/5.6
ISO	1600
FOCAL LENGTH	400MM
EXPOSURE	MANUAL

To avoid taking pictures of birds in cluttered backgrounds, wait for worm-eating birds to land on the ground.

Capturing

MOVEMENT

Portraying movement in wildlife photography is a balancing act. Ideally, you'll use a shutter speed slow enough to deliver a little motion blur, but not so slow that your image lacks clarity. Similarly, you want your images sharp, but if you freeze the action totally you might find your image loses its energy.

1 THINK FAST

Even if you want to show movement in your image with motion blur, you'll still want to use a reasonably quick shutter speed. Think 1/500th of a second at an absolute minimum, and much faster if you want to photograph small birds in flight: 1/2,000th and faster. If in doubt, raise the ISO on your camera rather than dropping the shutter speed to accommodate less-than-perfect light.

2 PAN

Holding your camera steady and waiting for an animal to cross the frame can be effective, but for fast-moving birds – such as the puffin on the opposite page – it's unlikely that your reactions will be fast enough. Follow your subject with your camera, pressing the shutter button as you pan across. If you pan at the same speed as your subject you'll get a sharp image and, with some luck, a photogenic blurred background.

3 BE CAREFUL WITH BURST MODES

Think of your camera's burst mode as a good way of getting a number of different framing options; your subject will be further forward in one frame, further back in another. However, careful timing is a better way of shooting a keeper: make sure your subject is focused before you start blasting away, rather than firing the shutter and hoping the lens will focus at some point in the sequence. If nothing else, being precise will cut down the number of images you have to edit when you get home.

■ AT-A-GLANCE SETTINGS

SHUTTER SPEED	1/1,000TH
APERTURE	F/8
ISO	1600
FOCAL LENGTH	400MM
EXPOSURE	+0.6

For fast-moving birds, such as puffins, try panning at the same speed as your subject to get a sharp image.

Using
AUTOFOCUS

If ever there was a double-edged sword for photographers, it's autofocus. On the one hand it keeps photography simple: in automatic mode, the lens will find the subject and lock the lens to it. On the other, there are many situations in which autofocus will miss, arrive late, or otherwise ruin your planned exposure – and unlike other mistakes, focus can't be corrected in software. Here's how to make autofocus work for you.

1 UNDERSTAND ITS WEAKNESSES

Autofocus is great at detecting and locking on to strongly defined subjects against plain backgrounds. Small birds against a backdrop of thin branches, however, will cause problems. Autofocus performance will also drop when you're shooting in low light. Knowing where your autofocus is likely to fall down is the first step to mastering it. In these situations, be ready to step in and flick your camera to manual focus.

2 USE SINGLE FOCUS POINTS

To give yourself a better chance, take your camera off its fully automatic mode. All cameras have a number of autofocus points, varying from around ten to more than 50. In automatic mode, your camera will look at the entire scene and try to pick out where the subject is in the frame, giving it plenty of scope for error. By manually selecting the autofocus point, you give the camera a much better chance of focusing accurately. This will also make you think about composition.

3 PRE-FOCUS

Think of autofocus as a semi-automatic feature. For instance, the picture on the right would have been impossible if fully automatic autofocus had been used: if the camera had tried to focus on the deer as it flashed across the frame, the animal would have been out of shot by the time the lens' motor had been driven to the right place. Instead, a previously leaping deer gave us something to focus on, and autofocus was left alone for the subsequent shot, because it was obvious the next deer was going to jump the stream at the same point.

▌ AT-A-GLANCE SETTINGS

SHUTTER SPEED	1/1,000TH
APERTURE	F/3.2
ISO	1250
FOCAL LENGTH	300MM
EXPOSURE	+0.6

By manually selecting your autofocus point, your camera is likely to focus more accurately.

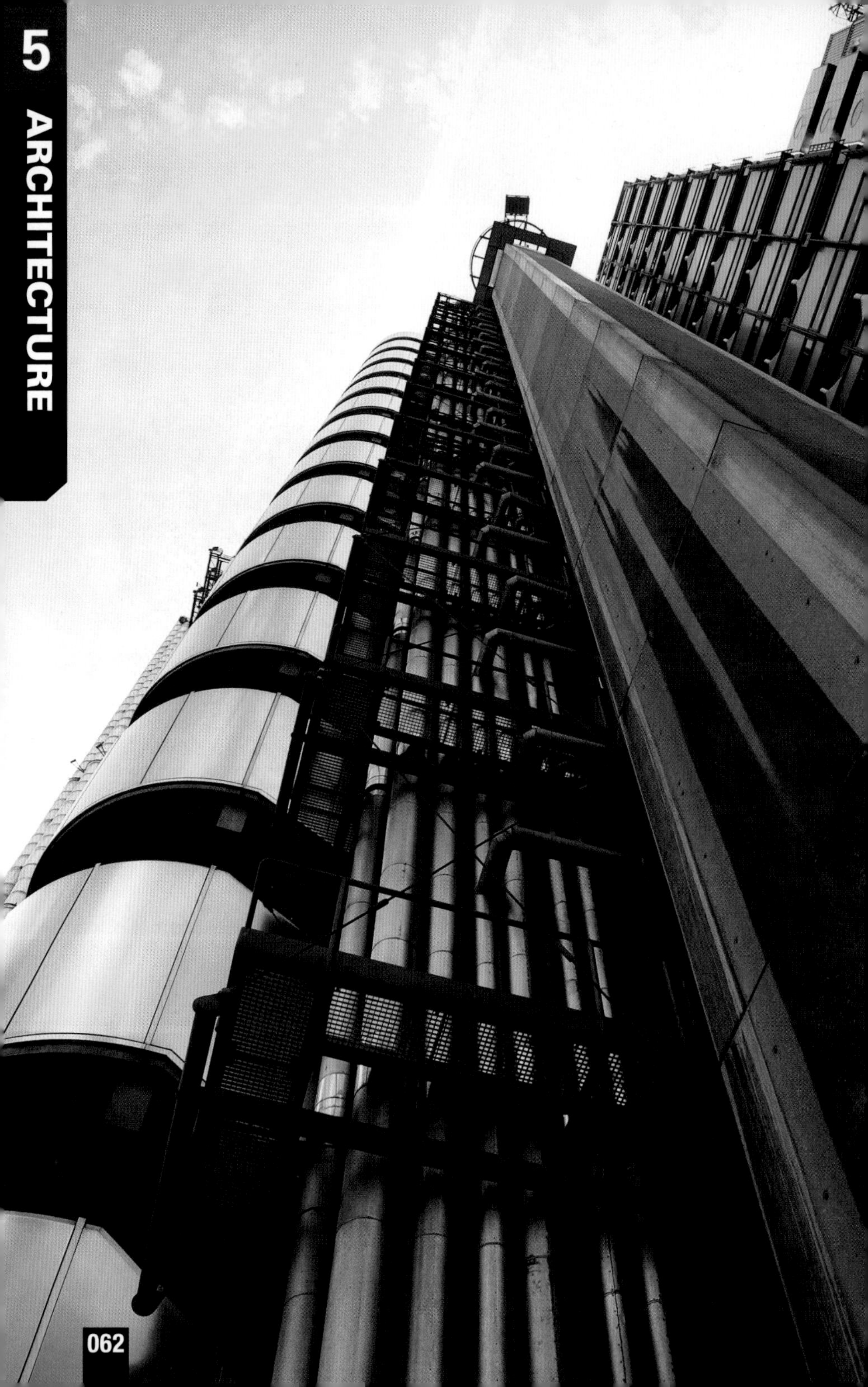

ARCHITECTURE

Grand, full of surprises and bursting with photographic possibilities: a modern city is a playground for photographers. From the highest skyscrapers of Dubai to the crumbling cathedrals of Central America, you have a great opportunity of grabbing a terrific shot no-one else has photographed before.

Best of all, architecture is an area of photography that requires virtually no specialised equipment. You don't need a particularly wide or long lens; if you're shooting during the day, you don't need an expensive lens with a large aperture either.

However, modern cities have their own problems. You'll be surrounded by people, and that's before you start to deal with some of the technical challenges of shooting upwards at tall buildings, or through the glass on sky-scraping observation decks. Read on to find out how to master the art.

064 In the bag

066 Shooting from high up

068 Taking photos of tall buildings

070 Adding impact by converting to black & white

IN THE BAG

While there are all sorts of gadgets and lenses you could use for photographing a city, the most important thing is a good eye – wherever you are, you'll probably be looking at something that thousands of others have already photographed, so you'll need to pick out a detail or an angle that nobody else has thought of before: think a close-up of the surface of the Eiffel Tower, or an ultra-low-angle shot of the Sydney Opera House.

If you want to make finding unique shots easier, you can opt to use more unusual lenses. For instance, you can correct perspective or add a toy-like effect to your images using a tilt-shift lens (see p42); alternatively, you could give a building a grand sense of scale by using an ultra wide-angle lens.

1 THRIFTY FIFTY

One of the most fun lenses any photographer can buy is a cheap 50mm f/1.8. These are available for virtually every camera platform, and are small, light and good value: less than £100 for a new one. On most cameras a 50mm lens produces a field of view similar to that of the human eye, which makes framing shots easy. The large aperture on these lenses means they're flexible too: you can opt for a small aperture for depth of field, or open up the lens to throw huge areas of the frame out of focus.

2 TILT-SHIFT LENS

These take practice, but are exceptionally sharp, and allow you to correct the kind of distortion you're likely to see when leaning up to take a picture of tall buildings. High vantage points can also be used with a

tilt-shift lens to create a vivid, if somewhat clichéd, toy effect, or you can "shift" the lens to change your eye point without needing something to stand on.

3 WIDE-ANGLE LENS

A wide-angle lens isn't useful for everyday photography. You can't really use it for taking shots of people, plus barrel distortion – where the horizon appears to bend up in the middle – can be difficult to avoid. But in cities, producing ultra-wide shots can help make views of often-photographed buildings look incredible.

4 DO I NEED A TRIPOD?

If you're shooting in the day, probably not. The best reason for carrying a tripod is that it will allow you to use long shutter speeds (1/15th of a second and slower), which could be useful if you're trying to maximise depth of field by using a small aperture, or if you're shooting at night. However, in good light you're unlikely to need one. In many cases – taking pictures of high-profile buildings, for instance – a tripod will attract the attention of overzealous security guards. Many skyscraper observation decks ban them.

Shooting from
HIGH UP

Nothing brings a new perspective to a location than shooting from overhead. By finding unusual, high-up vantage points, you'll be able to illustrate any city you visit in an interesting way that will put you far ahead of the postcards you can buy at the airport.

1 GO THROUGH THE GLASS CEILING

When you research your upwards trip, try to find somewhere that has an open-air balcony. Shooting through glass is tricky at the best of times, and if you're trying to press your camera against the glass through a throng of fellow holiday-makers, you'll have difficulty getting a decent shot.

2 DON'T DEPEND ON YOUR TRIPOD

The image to the right was taken as dusk was falling, but using a tripod wasn't an option. Many sky-high viewpoints, particularly in more safety-conscious countries, ban tripods outright. If you can't use a tripod, either try to find something to rest your camera on – a table, for example – or nudge the ISO upwards until you can use a shutter speed that produces a steady image. Remember that noise is easier to deal with than a blurred image!

This atmospheric image was taken at dusk, with a medium aperture of f/8 to get as much of the scene in focus as possible.

3 TIME YOUR VISIT

The middle of the day isn't a great time for photography. The sun is overhead and extremely bright, which makes getting interesting pictures tricky. It's also the busiest time of day for most tourist attractions, so getting a unique image will be more difficult. Try to arrive either just before the sun rises or just before it goes down to get the best light and the most interesting shots.

5

A fairly shallow angle has been used here, allowing us to get a reasonable amount of the view into the frame, while still giving a feeling of altitude.

▮ AT-A-GLANCE SETTINGS

SHUTTER SPEED	1/10TH
APERTURE	F/2.8
ISO	2000
FOCAL LENGTH	45MM
EXPOSURE	MANUAL

Taking pictures of

TALL BUILDINGS

Taking pictures of tall buildings is more difficult than it looks. Getting your perspective right is one challenge, another is taking an original shot. With skyscrapers frequently photographed, you need to think creatively about how you're composing, exposing and processing your shots if you want to stand out from the crowd.

1 PLAY WITH DEPTH OF FIELD

Skyscrapers are often photographed in their entirety, which makes for good record shots but often boring art. The building on the right was photographed from close range, at an aperture of f/8. That means the lower third of the building is sharply focused, but the top of the building begins to soften and blend into the sky, giving us a sense of scale that a fully focused shot might not.

2 PLAY WITH PERSPECTIVE

Using or hiring a tilt-shift lens (see p42) is a great way to add interest to your shots. Forget the faux toy-like effect you can generate, and experiment with the ability to place your camera's plane of focus – which normally lies flat across the middle of the frame – anywhere you like,

as well as being able to stop buildings appearing as though they're leaning away from the camera. The picture on the right was taken by looking up at the building. Using a tilt-shift lens means it looms much more, rather than falling away as it would if a normal lens had been used.

3 MOVE YOUR FEET!

If you find yourself repetitively pointing your camera up when taking photographs of architecture, it's likely your viewers will find themselves rubbing the backs of their necks as they put themselves in your shoes. Moving away from a cluster of skyscrapers and taking the photographs of them in the context of their surroundings is a great way of demonstrating scale, as well as allowing you to shoot with your camera level.

Using a tilt-shift lens to capture this building makes it look more looming, rather than as if it's falling away.

▌AT-A-GLANCE SETTINGS

SHUTTER SPEED	1/80TH
APERTURE	F/8
ISO	1000
FOCAL LENGTH	45MM
EXPOSURE	-0.6
TILT-SHIFT LENS	

Adding impact by converting to

BLACK & WHITE

Overcast skies? Don't stay inside! Shoot in colour now, and add interest by converting to black and white.

As a photographer, you're at the mercy of the weather. You can help yourself by trying to photograph during the "golden hour" – just after sunrise and just before sunset, when the light is at its warmest – but there will be times when that's impractical, or when the weather simply doesn't co-operate, delivering grey skies and flat, boring light.

Dull light doesn't necessarily mean dull photos, however. Converting a colour image to a high-contrast black and white one takes seconds, and can add an evocative and emotional tone to an image that colour often fails to convey. It's best to use a photo editor rather than the black and white setting on your camera for more control: Apple's Aperture and Adobe's Photoshop Elements are two powerful, good-value packages.

Even though you aren't shooting in black

■ AT-A-GLANCE SETTINGS

SHUTTER SPEED	1/15TH
APERTURE	F/16
ISO	400
FOCAL LENGTH	45MM
MONOCHROME CONVERSION IN ADOBE LIGHTROOM	

and white, it pays to think about how you'll process your images when you're taking them. Colour isn't important, but think instead about the relative brightness of objects and buildings in your shot; a good range of contrast will make a more interesting image. High-contrast black and white processing also benefits from a number of strong shapes and lines, which large cities have in abundance.

WINTER

There are few greater opportunities for photography than a good winter's day, which is why you should be outside at the first sign of snow starting to settle. Your favourite landscapes will be drastically altered, and scenes of enthusiastic tobogganists on your local slopes can produce classic images.

However, snow is a tricky customer to shoot. It presents unique challenges to your camera's metering system, for example, and you'll need to get the hang of exposure compensation if you want to avoid spending hours fiddling with your shots once you're back in front of your computer. You might also find that when faced with a snow-blanketed landscape, your camera's white balance starts to wander: this chapter will show you how to avoid both problems.

There are also hardware considerations to be aware of. On very cold days it's likely you'll subject your camera to temperatures outside the manufacturer's specifications. While this is unlikely to do any long-term damage to kit, you might find it's slower to respond.

074 In the bag
076 Getting exposure correct in the snow
078 Taking care of your gear in the cold
080 Correcting white balance

IN THE BAG

Given the amount of rain-proofing kit you can buy for your camera, it's surprising a similar accessory market hasn't sprung up for keeping it warm. Still, in terms of specific winter equipment, there isn't much you need: let your choice of kit be influenced by the thing you expect to shoot, not the temperature outside. That said, there are a few useful extras that could help.

1 FINGERLESS GLOVES

Your camera is a precision instrument, and the buttons and dials are designed to be used by dexterous human fingers, not clumsy gloved hands. If your gloves have exposed fingers – or better yet, mitten-style ends that can be rolled back – you'll be able to keep your hands warm without sacrificing the speed with which you operate your camera.

2 A JACKET WITH POCKETS

The only part of your camera that needs to be reasonably warm in order to work well is the battery. If it becomes cold you'll find that it runs out of juice pretty quickly. A jacket with lined pockets is the perfect place to store and warm up depleted cells.

3 HANDWARMER

Not only will these keep your batteries warm in your pockets (although make sure things don't get too hot), they're also a treat for photographers with chattering teeth.

Getting exposure correct in the

SNOW

However clever your camera may be, a few scenarios will always defeat it, and snow is a classic example. Here's how to get reliable exposures in the white stuff.

Your camera's exposure meter measures the brightness of a scene. This data is then used to set the exposure settings. The system works well when you're taking pictures of something that isn't very dark or bright, which is why a picture of a green landscape will expose correctly.

However, a snowy scene is extremely bright, and your camera's metering system is unlikely to handle this gracefully. Instead, it will be fooled into thinking the snow is a particularly bright object and, as a result, that it needs to shoot at a fast shutter speed to bring it down. If the snow in your image is made darker by a quick shutter speed, it will look muddy-grey in the final image; everything else in the image will be darker as well. Here's how to master it.

1 USE EXPOSURE COMPENSATION PART 1

Exposure compensation is useful when your camera is in a semi-automatic mode such as program or shutter priority. By using exposure compensation you can tell your camera to add or subtract a certain number of stops to what it thinks is the correct exposure. Set exposure compensation to -1, for instance, and it will take a shutter speed of 1/250th and increase it to 1/500th, so your image will be half as bright.

2 USE EXPOSURE COMPENSATION PART 2

As snow is white, your camera's reaction will be to increase the shutter speed to bring the whiteness down to a medium-grey. You want to force the camera to keep its exposures comparatively long, so set exposure to +1 to begin with. This means all your exposures will be twice as bright as your camera thinks they should be, which will mitigate its attempts to pull down the whiteness of snow.

3 EXPERIMENT

The beauty of digital is that you can check images and correct your settings based on what you see. On bright days, you might find adding a stop of exposure isn't enough: you may need as much as two extra stops to prevent under-exposure.

In this image, the snow is bright white, which is how it should look. Exposure compensation of +1 forced the shutter speed to 1/320th to keep things right.

▌ AT-A-GLANCE SETTINGS

SHUTTER SPEED	1/320TH
APERTURE	F/6.3
ISO	1600
FOCAL LENGTH	108MM
EXPOSURE	+1

Taking care of your gear in the

[COLD]

A DSLR camera is an amazingly complex blend of sensitive electrical circuitry and fragile mechanical components. Like any piece of equipment, if you use it incorrectly or expose it to hostile environments, you could ruin a crucial component and leave yourself open to a huge repair bill. Here's how to make sure your camera doesn't freeze to death.

This stunning Mongolian landscape was a doddle to shoot, but the camera batteries didn't like it.

▌AT-A-GLANCE SETTINGS

SHUTTER SPEED	1/250TH
APERTURE	F/5.6
ISO	100
FOCAL LENGTH	17MM
TEMPERATURE	-20° CELSIUS

1 KEEP DRY

Electronic devices don't particularly like the cold, but a much more serious problem is getting your camera wet, so beware condensation. When you take your gear from a cold place into a warm place – outdoors to inside, for instance – condensation droplets will form. Whatever happens, don't use your camera if it looks wet; leave it for around 20 minutes or so for the condensation to evaporate. If you see condensation on your camera, try not to take it outside again while there's water on it; the last thing you need is for that water to freeze, either inside or on the outside of your camera.

2 LOOK AFTER YOUR BATTERIES

Batteries become inefficient in the cold: you might find they run out of power quickly. The obvious solution is to keep a spare battery in your pocket. Failing that, if your fully charged battery fails after half an hour due to the cold, take it out of the camera and pop it into a pocket of one of your inner layers, or inside your glove. This will warm it up and restore it to life for a few dozen more shots.

3 BE BRAVE!

Most importantly, never chicken out of taking your camera with you because it's too cold. You didn't spend all that money on your kit to coddle it indoors!

■ AT-A-GLANCE SETTINGS

SHUTTER SPEED	1/640TH
APERTURE	F/4.5
ISO	800
EXPOSURE	+1.3
MANUAL WHITE BALANCE	

Correcting

WHITE BALANCE

White balance can go wrong even with the most expensive cameras, and snowy scenes are a particular Achilles' heel. Here's how to colour-correct your images in-camera and using software.

FIXING WHITE BALANCE IN SOFTWARE

If you shoot in RAW, fixing white balance after you've taken a shot is simple. In this instance, we've used Picasa (www.google.com/picasa), which is free, but the concepts are the same for most editing applications.

1 Double-click your image in Picasa's library, then click the Tuning tab towards the top left of the window. This is the Mac version, but the PC version looks identical.

2 At the bottom of the tool options you'll find the Neutral Color Picker. Click this, then select an area of your image that you know should be white. Click it, and the colour temperature of your image will be automatically adjusted. Alternatively, the Magic Wand tool to the right will attempt to correct colour balance automatically, although you may find you need to fine-tune things with the Color Temperature slider afterwards.

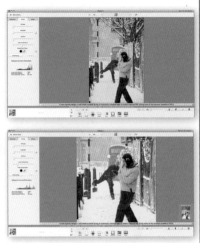

When your camera takes a picture, it attempts to determine the light it's working in, because different kinds of light dramatically affect the colour that objects appear. By accurately detecting the light in a shot, your camera knows what the white point is in your image. This ensures things that are white actually appear white. And, if white objects appear the correct colour, so will everything else.

All cameras will occasionally get white balance wrong. Cloudy days often trip up a camera; cloudy days alongside snow on the ground dramatically increase the odds of your camera miscalculating. The result? Blue snow and odd-looking skintones. Here's how to avoid it.

1 PRE-SET YOUR WHITE BALANCE

Look in your camera's manual to find out how to change the white balance. From the menu system, you can choose a variety of different light sources, such as a sunny day, a cloudy sky, or various indoor light sources such as tungsten or fluorescent lights. Picking one of these prevents your camera thinking for itself; which is useful when you know it's getting things wrong.

2 SET WHITE BALANCE MANUALLY

This involves taking a picture of something you know to be white. For example, if you take a picture of a piece of white paper and tell your camera to use that as a reference point, the white point in all your images will be the same as that sheet of paper. It's the best route if you want to be precise, but this takes a while to set up.

3 SHOOT IN RAW

Most edits you can make to your images involve losing a small amount of detail; not so when changing white balance. If you're editing a RAW file from your camera and you change the white balance, you don't lose any detail: it's essentially "free". Shooting RAW will burn through hard disk space more quickly, but you'll never need worry about what your camera is doing in terms of white balance when you're shooting.

SPORT

Photographing sports offers you the opportunity to create dynamic and exciting images, whether you're sitting on the Old Trafford sidelines or taking a picture of your local Sunday league team. Whatever calibre of sportspeople, you'll find plenty of incident to keep your camera engaged.

Simply turning up on the sidelines and snapping away is unlikely to get you anything worth keeping, though. If you want to take memorable shots, you'll need to invest in kit. A reasonably long telephoto lens is a good start, but for more ways to lighten your wallet and improve your photography, turn to p84.

The other ingredient is practice, and plenty of it. Framing shots of fast-moving athletes is tricky. Not only will you need good anticipation and reactions, but lots of experience with your lens to be able to get it trained and focused on a particular player more quickly. Turn to p88 for tips on getting your timing right.

Finally, note that you can't simply buy a ticket to a sporting event and turn up with your camera gear. Professional athletic organisations often retain copyright to any photos taken at their events, and some places won't even allow you in if you look too much like a pro. Instead, find a sport you want to photograph, and research amateur leagues in your area. A friendly phone call to arrange a visit will move you much closer to the action.

084 In the bag
086 How to show movement
088 Find a good position
090 Get your timing right

IN THE BAG

As with wildlife photography, taking pictures of sport is a demanding business. You can help yourself by practising and picking up the techniques in this chapter, but having the right kit will help too.

1 TELEPHOTO LENS

Unlike wildlife, athletes won't be scared off by your presence. Still, it's unlikely you'll be able to get too close, and the 18-55mm lens that came bundled with your camera won't cut it. Instead, opt for a lens with a decent focal length. For many sports, 70-300mm is a good choice: the ability to zoom in and out will compensate for those times when you're unable to change your position. For sports with large areas of play, such as football, a longer lens will be useful. Something as long as 400mm is a good start, and a 500mm lens should cover all eventualities. Just note this will cost much more.

2 FAST TELEPHOTO LENS

Having a long lens is one thing; a fast lens quite another. Most consumer telephotos have a maximum aperture of f/5.6 at their longest setting. That's fine on a sunny day, but not much use for indoor or floodlit sports. For instance, if you're feeling flush you could opt for something along the lines of the Canon 200mm f/2: a prime lens that has a sensationally large aperture. This means it's big and expensive, but perfectly suited to sports photography.

3 MONOPOD FOR ABOVE

A fast telephoto lens is a heavy piece of kit. While most adults will be able to heft one up to their eye level, holding it there for any length of time in anticipation of a shot requires strong shoulders. Using a monopod for sports photography is better than using a tripod: it's portable, making changing position easier. It also makes pivoting the camera easier, allowing you to react faster.

4 WIRELESS FLASH TRIGGER

If you can gain permission to use an external light, being able to trigger your off-camera flash wirelessly could create sensational results. Devices such as those made by PocketWizard (**www.pocketwizard.com**) transmit exposure information from your camera to your flash, allowing you to light the action from whatever angle you choose. You can even use multiple flashes. Expect to spend a few hundred pounds for a basic setup, though, and remember to ask permission before leaving tripods and flashguns around the edges of the field!

5 RAIN JACKET FOR CAMERA

Some sports get under way whatever the weather. While this could involve sitting in the rain for hours, sports such as hockey and rugby offer spectacular photo opportunities as the players struggle to get to grips with muddy conditions. Protect your camera gear from the wet weather with a dedicated rain jacket. Using a coat designed specifically for DSLRs will allow you quick access to your camera's controls.

1

2

3

4

5

How to show

MOVEMENT

Demonstrating movement in a photograph takes work to perfect.
Practice is the most effective approach, but here's where to start.

Panning the camera while the shutter was open, plus the movement of the cyclists, has created a dynamic image.

racetrack will simply look like it's parked. To evoke a sense of action in your images, you need to tread the line between a shutter speed that's too slow, and one that's too fast.

1 PAN THE CAMERA

The photograph on the left was taken by panning the camera – perhaps the most important aspect of demonstrating speed in a photograph. With your camera focusing precisely on your target, follow it with your camera and keep it in the same place in your viewfinder. Without stopping your movement, push the shutter button. Since your subject isn't moving relative to the camera, it will appear sharp; but because the background is moving relative to the camera, it will look like it's whizzing past in a blur.

2 EXPERIMENT WITH SHUTTER SPEEDS

On an overcast day, you may have no choice but to use a slow shutter speed. This is good, because you'll be forced into practising your panning. On bright days, or with bright lenses, the temptation will be to set a particularly fast shutter speed to ensure crisp, shake-free images. Instead, start with your camera at 1/500th of a second and see what kind of results you get. Use shutter-priority mode and allow your camera to set the aperture to keep life simple.

3 ZOOM!

If you find yourself with fast-moving subjects coming towards you, you won't be able to pan. Instead, to demonstrate movement, try zooming out slightly as you take a picture. Give your lens' zoom ring a quick twist as you press the shutter button. The change in focal length will be captured in the final image as a blur.

Freezing the action in sports photography is easy. Set your camera to aperture-priority mode and choose a large aperture (f/5.6 or bigger), then raise the sensitivity of your camera's sensor by increasing the ISO to 800 or higher. Unless you're shooting in the dark, the camera will be forced to choose a fast shutter speed. For most sports, a speed of 1/1,500th of a second will result in pin-sharp images.

Totally frozen images aren't always ideal, though, because you risk sterilising the action. For example, a totally frozen car on a

Find a good

POSITION

In all photography, finding a good position is key. The calibre of your kit will be unimportant if you have to shoot through crowds of people, or if you're so far away from the action that the participants are distant blurs. For that reason, forget taking your camera to Premier League games or high-end sporting events – you'll never be close enough to take a decent shot. Until you start accumulating press passes, follow these instructions to find the best vantage points.

1 GET AS CLOSE AS YOU CAN

No matter how long it is, your telephoto lens is almost certainly best deployed as near to the action as possible. By moving closer, you'll be able to fill the frame better. And, by staking your claim to the best vantage point early, you can move backwards and forwards more easily.

2 TAKE RISKS

Your camera is insured, right? The picture on the right was taken in knee-deep seawater, but moving backwards to the safety of the beach would have meant a much less distinct shot.

3 GET PLENTY OF ANGLES

Spending your entire shoot in one place is the easiest approach, especially if you're carrying heavy kit with you, but hundreds of shots from the same angle will get boring. Keep your eyes peeled for better positions and try not to spend too long in the same place.

■ AT-A-GLANCE SETTINGS

SHUTTER SPEED	1/1,000TH
APERTURE	F/7.1
ISO	200
FOCAL LENGTH	300mm
EXPOSURE	TV

A telephoto lens won't magically enlarge your subjects to fill the frame; you need to move your feet too.

DANGER SHOT

Get your

TIMING RIGHT

Timing is key in photography, but never more so than when shooting a sporting event. Moments of interest come and go in a matter of seconds, so you'll need to anticipate what's going to happen in order to be ready: once you've missed a great frame you may never have the chance to catch it again.

1 ANTICIPATE THE ACTION

Anticipation is better than reaction. Shooting sports you've never watched before will always be challenging, simply because you don't know what's coming next. Do your homework and try to anticipate key moments, and be ready for them. For instance, the shot on the right shows a volleyball serve. By watching the player for a few points it became easy to predict where she would be in the frame when serving, resulting in a well-composed, sharp image.

2 FRAME SHOTS IN YOUR HEAD FIRST

Trying to follow action through a camera viewfinder is difficult; more so when using a long focal length, because your subject can move out of frame fast. Instead, watch the action without keeping your eye pressed to the viewfinder, and compose shots when something interesting happens.

3 USE YOUR CONTINUOUS MODE INTELLIGENTLY

Sticking your fancy DSLR on its continuous burst mode and blasting away is an impulse to be resisted. For one thing, the amount of work you'll have to do choosing and discarding images on your computer will be massively increased. Second, all cameras have a buffer: the number of images that can be captured before the camera needs to take a break to process and store the data it has gathered. This number goes down if you're shooting RAW files, and continuously firing the shutter might mean your camera is processing when something truly interesting happens.

■ AT-A-GLANCE SETTINGS

SHUTTER SPEED	1/1,000TH
APERTURE	F/10
ISO	400
FOCAL LENGTH	70MM
EXPOSURE	+/-0

Anticipating the action by paying attention to what's happening will result in a well-composed shot.

INDOOR

Taking pictures outdoors is easy. On a day with blue skies, your images will naturally need fast exposure times, and your camera's focusing system will be more effective because of the ample light. The result? Sharp images that need minimal adjustment later in terms of white balance, exposure or sharpness.

Inside, it's a different matter. Not only is there less light but the quality of the light, in terms of tint and direction, will be radically different. This means the kit you use may change, and your camera settings definitely will. You'll need to understand the impact of different ISO settings on both shutter speeds and image quality.

This chapter covers lighting still-life subjects (see p104) and macro subjects, to working with virtually no light at all; you'll soon be able to reliably wield a camera whether you're shooting in a well-equipped home studio or at an evening party.

We'll also look into music photography, a genre in which you could find yourself working in good light, no light and strangely coloured light all in the space of two minutes. Read on to find out how to master it.

094 In the bag
096 Using light indoors
098 Using ISO
100 Good party photography
101 Photograph action indoors
102 Taking photos at gigs
104 Still life

IN THE BAG

Taking good pictures indoors requires thought. Shooting outdoors more or less guarantees a reasonable supply of predictable light; when you're inside, you can take total control. If you don't have access to an external light, you'll need to have a look at your selection of lenses. If you don't want to start pushing up the ISO, a large lens with a fast maximum aperture will help get light on to the sensor and keep shutter speeds fast.

1 LIGHTS

It's likely you have at least one room in your house that gets plenty of light. This is useful, but for maximising the amount of time during the day (or night) that you can shoot, external lights are indispensable. For maximum portability, a Speedlight (Speedlite for Canon users) can be attached to your camera's hotshoe, or used off-camera with a dedicated cable or wireless system.

For more power, consider a studio lighting system: consumer-level systems can be bought for less than £150 from reputable retailers. A studio lighting system is powered by the mains, and can often be set to provide a constant supply of bright, even-temperature lighting; useful if you're setting up a still-life and don't want to wait until you fire the flash to make sure there are no odd shadows. It can also be handy for portraiture, as your subject will have time to get used to the light rather than being blinded when the flash goes off.

2 MACRO LENS

If you're working with a set of lights, you'll be able to get away with a lens of just about any maximum aperture; for some subjects, however, the minimum focusing distance could be an issue. To ensure small subjects fill the frame, consider a dedicated macro lens (Nikon calls these micro lenses). The 105mm lens pictured has a long focal length, but will focus on something only 12in from its front element – great for depicting fine detail or abstracting common objects.

3 FAST TELEPHOTO

If you want to use a telephoto lens indoors, choose one with a fast aperture. Many such consumer lenses have a maximum aperture of f/5.6 or slower when zoomed in – fine in good weather outside, but not much use indoors. Using long focal lengths inside requires technical proficiency and decent kit. This Canon lens is expensive but offers superb optical quality, and a f/2.8 aperture.

4 FAST BUDGET LENS

If you'd rather keep your camera bill into three figures – or less – most camera manufacturers make fast fixed focal length lenses. The Sony (right) has a focal length of 35mm, which is great for portraits, and a maximum aperture of f/1.8. This allows you to create interesting depth-of-field effects, as well as allowing lots of light onto the sensor.

8

1

2

3

4

USING LIGHT
indoors

Certain aspects of indoor photography can be corrected on a PC, but ensuring images are as good as they can be in-camera will be beneficial. Part of this is learning how to use an off-camera flash, but noting the light that's already available will be a huge help. Not only will this inform how you use your flash, it also means you'll be better prepared when your flash batteries inevitably die just as you're getting into the swing of things.

1 SHOOT IN MANUAL

The image on the right was a challenge. Not only were there bars to shoot through, but the light was both very low and a deep orange colour. Using a flash was out of the question to avoid annoying the subject: never a good idea with a 20-stone tiger, regardless of which side of the fence it's on. The first thing to do is shoot in manual

mode to avoid the camera's exposure system stepping in – the risk of confusion goes up in poor light. We needed a fast shutter speed to stop the tiger blurring, and a large aperture to get plenty of light in. We used a 70-200mm lens with a fast maximum aperture of f/2.8 to get the brightest results, while a shutter speed of 1/250th guaranteed a shake-free image whatever the lens' focal length.

2 KNOW YOUR CAMERA

Low ISO settings are useless indoors unless your camera is on a tripod and your subject is still. Here, the demands of setting a fast exposure coupled with the poor light meant a very high ISO to get enough light to create an image: we used ISO 6400. Many cameras don't offer this setting; some that do produce unusably poor images. The best advice is to get used to your camera beforehand, and know its limit ahead of time. In the event you're faced with getting a noisy image versus not getting an image at all, however, don't be afraid to ramp up the ISO settings.

3 MIND WHITE BALANCE

Just because your images aren't radically off-colour, it doesn't mean you don't need to adjust white balance afterwards. Shoot in RAW to allow for editing.

■ AT-A-GLANCE SETTINGS

SHUTTER SPEED	1/250TH
APERTURE	F/2.8
ISO	6400
FOCAL LENGTH	80MM
EXPOSURE	MANUAL

USING ISO

Along with shutter speeds and aperture, the ability to understand and quickly access the ISO setting on your camera is crucial to creating great photos in challenging situations.

ISO determines how much your sensor reacts to light. A low number means it's less sensitive, and that calls for a slower shutter speed or larger aperture, and vice versa. Adding sensitivity isn't free, however: the more sensitive your camera, the more noise you'll see. Expensive cameras with larger sensors are less prone to noise, but it's a universal fact of digital photography.

1 KNOW YOUR LIMITS

Just because your camera shoots at ISOs up to 25,600, doesn't mean you should use it. When you first get your camera spend a few days shooting unimportant subjects at various ISO settings, and inspect them on your computer or, even better, once they've been printed out. This way, you'll be able to judge which ISO setting is the safe maximum that still returns usable shots.

2 THINK IN STOPS

Each time you double your camera's ISO, you halve the necessary exposure. That means ISO 200 is twice as sensitive as ISO 100, and requires either half the shutter speed, or half the aperture size to return the same exposure. Working with

ISO in full manual mode presents a real challenge, but once you can do it you'll find far fewer missed exposures.

3 USE NOISE REDUCTION

Many cameras offer in-camera noise reduction, but this is less effective when shooting RAW files, and is something of a blunt tool. However, most photo-editing packages offer superior noise-reduction tools. If in doubt, shoot a "safe" exposure time to gain a steady image, and use a higher ISO. Reducing noise is possible in software: reducing camera shake is not!

Resting the camera on the rail provided some stability, but a very high ISO was used to keep the shutter speed below a second.

▊ AT-A-GLANCE SETTINGS

SHUTTER SPEED	0"6
APERTURE	F/5.6
ISO	2800
FOCAL LENGTH	14MM
EXPOSURE	MANUAL

PARTY
photography

Now you're a dab hand with a camera, you'll quickly find yourself relied upon to take pictures at parties. These two simple tips will help ensure you capture great shots, without getting in the way.

1 USE A FLASH

Lighting is often dim at parties. Being able to control the light falling on your subjects with an external flash will allow you to make sure everyone in the frame is evenly lit. Don't rely on the flash on your camera – use an external flash, and either fire it from off the camera, or bounce it off the ceiling for more natural-looking light.

2 BE CANDID

There are plenty of people who freeze when you point a camera at them. Catching folk acting naturally will mean a more relaxed shot, and may even make it look like people were having fun. For this kind of photography, using a longer lens will allow you to catch people enjoying a joke from across the room without them noticing you.

Photographing action
INDOORS

Photographing action anywhere is demanding, but moving indoors places even more strain on your kit and technique. Lighting is often the biggest change, with the natural light of the sun replaced by dim overhead lights. You might find your subjects are lit by multiple lights at once, all coming from different directions. You might find there's a single source of light from one side. Staying aware of how much light you have to play with, and where it's coming from, is the best way to guarantee a good shot.

1 FORGET YOUR FLASH
In most situations, you'll be too far from the action for even the most powerful flashes to have an impact. This means you have little choice but to go for step 2.

2 RAISE ISO
No flash means using the available light. At professional events, interior lighting will easily be enough to shoot at ISOs around 800 and still get usable shutter speeds. If you haven't invested in a camera yet, or you're thinking about upgrading, then high ISO performance is one of the crucial aspects to look out for.

3 MONITOR WHITE BALANCE
Complicated lighting indoors has the potential to trip up your camera's white balance. If in doubt, shoot in

RAW mode and correct the white balance afterwards. Turn to p80 for more on adjusting white balance.

Taking photos at

GIGS

Capturing live music with all its energy is one of the most challenging kinds of photography there is. The amount of light varies tremendously from second to second, both in brightness and colour, plus the people you're photographing dash around on stage, meaning you need a quick shutter speed to freeze them. And that's before you consider the hundreds of other people...

1 GET TO THE FRONT

It's possible to take intimate portraits of performers at gigs, but to do so you'll need to frame people's faces tightly. The best way to do this is through a combination of a long telephoto lens and old-fashioned muscle: get to the front if you can, although arranging access to the photography pit – if there is one – is your best bet.

2 THINK ABOUT THE LIGHT

Where is the light coming from? How bright is it? The lights might come up at the end of every song, allowing you to grab a few well-lit portraits of the performers while they tune their instruments or talk to the crowd. If a performer is being lit strongly from one side, try to position yourself on the lit side for a useful portrait, or the opposite side for a backlit silhouette effect.

3 MASTER YOUR ISO

Inevitably, some gigs are going to be better lit than others, so you need to know how to raise the ISO of your camera, and be able to do it quickly. The image on the right was taken at ISO 1600, for instance, and while that means higher noise, it's preferable to have a sharp, noisy image than a blurred clean one. Try to keep your ISO as low as possible – adjust it as the light changes throughout the set.

4 UP THE SPEED

If you simply want sharp photos, use your camera's shutter priority mode and set it to 1/400th of a second or faster. Even if there isn't enough light, your camera will freeze the action, although it will produce an under-exposed image. Don't ignore the creative possibilities of motion blur, though.

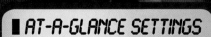

▮ AT-A-GLANCE SETTINGS

SHUTTER SPEED	1/90TH
APERTURE	F/4.8
ISO	1600
FOCAL LENGTH	80MM
EXPOSURE	AUTO

When taking photos at gigs, keep an eye on where the light is coming from. Varying your position will mean you end up with well-lit portraits and those with a silhouette effect.

STILL LIFE

With a little care and technique, you can turn the trinkets and curios in your house into amazing photos. If you have a resident antique hoarder, now's the time to start pilfering their treasure chest in search of something with fine detail, interesting lines or vivid colours. Good still-life subjects can be found all over the house – virtually every room will have something that's interesting from at least one angle. And, once you've learned the basics of lighting and focusing, there will be no stopping you.

1 LIGHTING IS EVERYTHING

Look around you in the room you want to shoot in. Where does the light come from? How big are the windows? When is the room in direct sunlight: once a day for an hour or so, or for a prolonged period in the afternoon? If your house has large French windows, and you have a reasonably fast lens, you might be able to shoot with only natural light.

The shot on the right, however, was taken in a relatively dark, west-facing room with little sunlight. Due to this, an external, off-camera flash was fired from above the subject to produce enough light.

Using an off-camera flash allows you to determine exactly where the shadows will fall in your image: you can light a subject from above, or from beneath to create an intimidating up-lit effect.

2 BACKGROUND

Popping your still-life subject on the kitchen table and firing away is the easy approach, but it isn't the best. Most art shops sell large sheets of coloured paper – pick up a range of colours, and see which best complements your subject's tones. Arrange your background so it falls vertically behind your subject, then curves under it – this will make the background undistracting and seamless. Here we used a large sheet of slightly off-white background paper.

3 FIND DETAILS TO PHOTOGRAPH

Photographing your subject as a whole is great for eBay, but when shooting still life, allowing your shots to trail out of the frame adds interest. Move as close as you can to make the most of fine details; a macro lens is good for this.

AT-A-GLANCE SETTINGS

SHUTTER SPEED	1/200TH
APERTURE	F/6.3
ISO	100
FOCAL LENGTH	190mm
FLASH	EXTERNAL

Make your still-life photos interesting by taking shots from various angles; move in close to capture fine detail.

NIGHT

Some environments come alive after dark. Cities take on dangerous and interesting new personalities, and daylight gives way to a fascinating variety of mixed-colour light sources. Pay attention, and you'll find as much to photograph at night as during the day.

Taking pictures during the day is taxing enough, but striving for perfect images after sunset adds a new layer of technical difficulty. With less light, you either need to work with long shutter times, or start sending your camera's ISO through the roof to get bright images. Both have their pitfalls in terms of image quality, but with careful application of the tricks featured in this chapter, you'll be able to produce interesting, sharp images whatever the light.

We'll also cover the kit you need (see p108): a tripod is useful for some night photography (see p111), but it isn't a must-have. If you know how to use the ISO setting on your camera (see p116), you'll be able to shoot surprisingly good images at night without using any support at all. Read on to find out how to double the number of hours in the day you can use your camera.

108 In the bag
110 Using exposure to create light trails
112 Using tripods
114 Shooting handheld

IN THE BAG

Photographing at night might be tricky, but you can help yourself by being prepared. Leave the telephoto lens at home, for instance, and stick to wide-angle optics for steadier shots. Here's our list of indispensable night-time camera gear.

1 FULL-FRAME CAMERA

Brace yourself, because this is going to set you back a pretty penny. But if you want professional-quality images from your night shots, a full-frame camera will give you the best bang-per-buck in terms of ISO performance. The large sensor at its heart means its photosensors are further apart, so they interfere less with each other as they warm up during a long exposure. The result? Good-looking shots, even as you push the ISO into the thousands.

2 TRIPOD

You won't always need it, but it's a must for light-trail shots, or taking pictures of the cosmos. If you have a relatively light camera you don't need to spend a lot of money, but note that the cheapest tripods are a poor match for bigger cameras and lenses. Pay attention to the weight limit of any tripod you look at buying.

3 REMOTE SHUTTER RELEASE

These take two forms: you can either use a cable release, which plugs into your camera directly, or a cheap infrared remote. Most DSLRs support these, and pressing the button will autofocus your camera and fire the shutter. The benefit is that you don't have to touch your camera while the shutter

is open, which leads to a steadier image. Wireless remotes are also very cheap: you'll easily be able to pick one up for less than £20.

4 THERMOS

It's cold at night, and your instinct will be to get back indoors as soon as possible. Extend the time you can comfortably wait around with a hot drink (dash of whisky optional), and increase your chance of being present for that perfect frame.

5 WIDE-ANGLE, STABILISED LENS

A wide-angle lens not only allows you to take landscapes at night, but the wide focal length will be less susceptible to shaking hands. The pictured lens has a focal length of only 15mm at its widest, and an image stabiliser as well, making it perfect for handheld, night-time photography.

6 MOBILE PHONE

Night photography in urban areas isn't necessarily dangerous, but it pays to have your wits about you, particularly in isolated places such as motorway bridges. Take a friend, if possible; at the very least make sure you're out of the way of traffic and can contact someone in the event of a mishap.

Using long exposure to create
LIGHT TRAILS

Your local motorway overpass might not strike you as a setting rich with photographic possibilities, but it's a superb place to learn how to work with long shutter speeds.

With most of your photography, a blurry image is one that's best sent to the recycle bin forever. Blurry images are stressful to look at, as the eye keeps hunting for a detail to lock on to.

However, by understanding motion, and how light affects a camera's sensor, you can use long exposures to create a feeling of speed and movement in your images. The example on the right – streaks of motorway traffic at night – has become something of a stereotype, but there are lots of applications elsewhere. Think fairgrounds, airports, even the stars in the sky: anywhere with bright, well-defined, moving light sources is a candidate.

1 KEEP STEADY
Although you want some parts of your image to be blurred, it's no good if the whole thing is shaky. You'll generally be shooting for periods far longer than a second, which is more than you'll be able to handhold a camera. To make sure your scene is steady, a tripod, or at least somewhere flat and steady where you can rest your camera, is a must.

2 FOCUSING IN THE DARK
The shot on the right used an aperture of f/11. The shutter speed isn't really important: we know it has to be long, so it's worth making sure your shot has minimal depth of field. Not only will the final image be sharp all over, but it means you can be a little less precise when focusing.

3 SHUTTER SPEEDS
The ten-second exposure here works well, as there's enough traffic passing through to make the shot look busy. At busier periods, a faster shutter speed and higher ISO would work. If it's quiet, you'll need a longer shutter speed so the streaks of traffic look interesting. Keep the aperture the same, and adjust ISO and shutter speed to expose your shot.

▌AT-A-GLANCE SETTINGS

SHUTTER SPEED	10"
APERTURE	F/11
ISO	400
FOCAL LENGTH	23MM
EXPOSURE	MANUAL

The use of a tripod here ensures that blur is present only where you want it; the rest of the image remains sharp.

Using a

TRIPOD

A tripod isn't essential for most photography. The only reason you need one during daylight hours is if you're using a long shutter speed to create a particular effect: using an ND filter to blur a waterfall, for instance (see p142). However, when you're photographing at night, being able to support your camera without touching it is extremely useful. These tips will help you make the most out of your three-legged friend.

1 BEWARE OF SHAKE

Your camera is already protected from shake by the tripod, right? Not quite. Even the simple act of pressing the shutter button on your camera will shake the sensor enough to introduce blur to your image. Avoid this by using a cheap remote control (less than £20 for a wireless one). If you forget yours, or don't fancy spending the cash, look in the manual to see if your camera has a two-second self-timer. The shot on the right was taken using this method.

2 A TRIPOD ONLY STEADIES THE CAMERA, NOT THE SUBJECT

Sometimes, as with photographing moving traffic (see p110), you'll want motion blur in your images. Other moving objects, such as people or even relatively slow-moving objects, will look as though they're dashing around in the final shot. If you're photographing a person, make sure they know to remain still until the image is taken.

3 KEEP AN EYE ON IT

Your tripod might look steady as a rock, but it could still be decidedly top-heavy, particularly if you've upgraded your camera to a decent model and haven't got round to upgrading your tripod. A decent knock from just the right direction could send it toppling. If in doubt, keep your camera's strap around your neck as a failsafe.

The act of pressing the shutter button is enough to introduce blur to your images; use a tripod to steady your camera.

■ AT-A-GLANCE SETTINGS

SHUTTER SPEED	13"
APERTURE	F/11
ISO	400
FOCAL LENGTH	23mm
EXPOSURE	-2

Shooting
HANDHELD

Shooting at night is the obvious time to put your tripod to use, but there will be times when this isn't practical.

Some photographic opportunities are fleeting, and by the time you've assembled your tripod with the camera on top, the moment will be gone. At other times, you'll need to follow the action; another area in which tripods aren't great. Shooting handheld at night requires some juggling, but once you're confident shooting in low light, there will be no stopping you.

1 LEARN YOUR MINIMUM SHUTTER SPEED

This depends on the lens you're using. A ground rule is that your slowest shutter speed is one over the focal length: 1/50th of a second for a 50mm lens, for example. However, you may well be steady enough to shoot slower than that if you're careful; if your lens is stabilised, you may find up to four extra stops of stability. So, on a 17mm lens you may be able to shoot an exposure as low as half a second before camera shake

becomes a threat. At this speed, your challenge will be convincing your subject to stay still. The picture on the right was taken handheld at only 1/5th of a second.

2 BREATHE

Whether or not you have image stabilisation, your body's movement while taking a shot will have an impact. Before taking a long handheld exposure, take a deep breath and frame your shot. As you exhale, push the shutter button. Continue to exhale until the shutter snaps closed again.

3 PAY ATTENTION TO THE LIGHT

The shot on the right was easy: it's a photograph, essentially, of a group of lights. In other photographs, make sure your subject is well lit. Move groups of friends under streetlamps to get more light to fall on them, for example. If you're photographing a building, wait until the floodlights are turned on before you shoot it!

▮ AT-A-GLANCE SETTINGS

SHUTTER SPEED	1/5TH
APERTURE	F/4
ISO	100
FOCAL LENGTH	17MM
FLASH	MANUAL

UNDERWATER

Just when you thought you had the subtleties of photography in the bag, underwater photography turns everything you know on its head. Not only will you have to invest in new kit and learn how to use it, but you'll need to marry proficient diving abilities with technical photographic ability if you want to resurface with decent images.

Once you've read this chapter, you'll know what to look out for when in deep waters. Whether it's being aware of the colour-correction you'll need to carry out once you have your images (see p122), or of backscatter (see p126) and the need to keep your subjects close, this chapter will give you a head start.

Practice makes perfect, though, and there's no better way to refine your technique than by heading to your nearest diving spot and experimenting. The UK is a tough place to start: dark skies and little life near the surface means the most interesting spots tend to be deeper, so you'll need to be a qualified diver to get under way. Head abroad, however, and amazing coral reefs make it next to impossible to surface with dull shots; the Mediterranean and Egypt are both teeming with life and only a few hours from the UK.

Finally, a word on safety. Diving, even snorkelling, is potentially dangerous, and your kit and photography should be secondary considerations to your safety. Whether it's getting charged by a trigger fish or keeping an eye on your buoyancy, there are plenty of ways to get into trouble underwater without becoming distracted by your aperture settings.

118 In the bag
120 Using underwater housings
122 Editing underwater photos
124 Using lenses underwater
126 Backscatter & underwater lighting

IN THE BAG

When it comes to taking images underwater, there are two ways to approach the kit you need: the cheap way and the proper way. The cheap way includes PVC pouches designed to be used at shallow depths. While these work, they're not ideal for serious photographers.

PVC pouches are one-size-fits-all, which means getting at the controls on your camera is fiddly. They also trap huge amounts of air, making the resulting kit incredibly buoyant – and diving next to impossible. Even snorkelling at more than a few feet becomes difficult.

1 COMPACT CAMERA AND CASE

Proper hard-shell cases are almost neutrally buoyant, which makes them easy to dive with. They're also built for specific models of camera, which means they come with dials that connect directly to your camera's physical controls, allowing you to change settings underwater.

To start with, consider using a compact camera. A top-end model such as the Canon S95 will set you back around £300, and its corresponding underwater case another £200. The result is a camera waterproof to 40 metres.

2 DSLR CASE

Once you gain some experience, the next step will be to invest in an underwater case for your DSLR. It's here that you'll start to spend serious cash. On an entry-level DSLR such as the Nikon D3100, an Ikelite housing will set you back around £1,000 – nearly three times the cost of the camera.

If you own a Canon 7D, for example, expect to spend £1,200 – and more again if you own a full-height body such as a Nikon D3s. American outfit Ikelite is well regarded and makes cases for most current DSLR models.

3 INSURANCE

Finally, your existing household insurance won't cover underwater photography. In fact, it's unlikely that even dedicated camera insurance will cover you for water ingress, although it will often cover underwater equipment on land. If your camera gets wet, particularly with salt water, it's unlikely you'll be able to save it. Make absolutely certain you have insurance that covers you for an expensive, and probably irreparable, technical failure. Online communities such as **www.wetpixel.com** will be able to provide advice on which companies can help.

1

2

Using underwater

HOUSINGS

Once you've chosen your underwater housing, getting to grips with it will take a little practice. If you've chosen wisely, your housing will offer access to all your camera's normal controls; key features, such as focusing and metering, won't be affected either. Life isn't as simple as locking your camera in its housing and diving in, though.

1 BEWARE GLARE

If you're taking pictures near the surface, you might find that the LCD on the back of your camera is all but unusable since it will reflect so much light. This means using it to frame shots will be a hit and miss affair, and the best approach in this situation is to forget everything you've learned about timing: simply set your camera to continuous mode and take lots of images. Those using a DSLR housing will be at an advantage here, since they can use its optically perfect viewfinder.

2 TAKE CARE OF CONDENSATION

Silica gel is supplied with underwater housings. It's intended to stay in your underwater housing with your camera, and will absorb any moisture that accumulates as a result of condensation. It doesn't offer protection against leaks, however: the best way to protect your equipment from this is to make a point of checking your waterproof housing before every use. This includes such things as checking the rubber O-ring seal that keeps water out and replacing it if it's cracked or degrading, as well as washing your kit with fresh water once you've finished diving.

3 READ THE MANUAL

Finally, keep the instruction manual! Failing to read the instruction booklet that was supplied with your camera might hold you back technically, but ignoring the instructions relating to your underwater kit could result in a far more expensive failure.

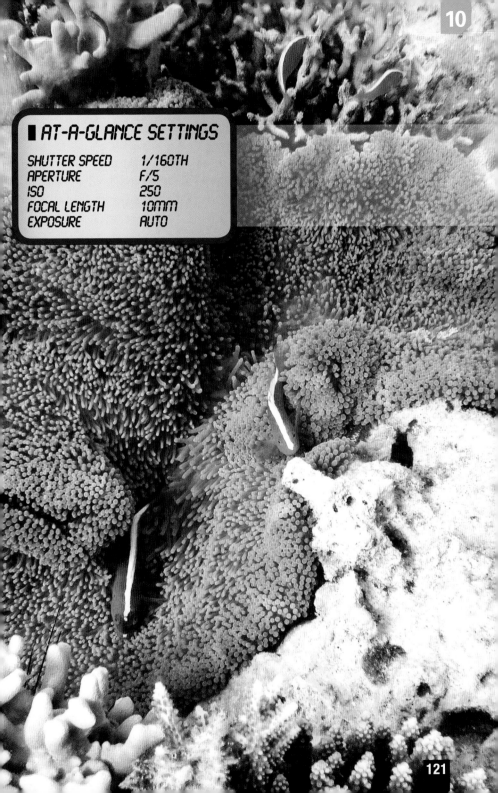

■ AT-A-GLANCE SETTINGS

SHUTTER SPEED	1/160TH
APERTURE	F/5
ISO	250
FOCAL LENGTH	10MM
EXPOSURE	AUTO

EDITING
underwater photos

As we'll see on p126, taking pictures underwater creates great technical challenges, with the effect water has on light one of the biggest. On a cloudy day, you'll lose around two stops of light the minute you slip beneath the waves, and water also absorbs certain wavelengths, which will result in photographs with a much cooler white balance. Here's how to save your images and restore them to their full glory.

1 BE CONSCIOUS OF WHITE BALANCE

Many popular compact cameras have a dedicated underwater setting in the white balance menu, which should help produce correct colours. If your camera doesn't have one (most DSLRs don't), setting white balance manually using a card will be far too much hassle. Instead, shoot in RAW and set white balance later. As a rule of thumb, you'll want your shots to be warmer than your camera shot them.

Software such as Adobe Lightroom allows you to change the tint of your shot, which can help tone down images with too much green in them.

2 ADD CONTRAST

Images recorded underwater require you to be more heavy handed with your image editor. Even images taken with expensive, contrast lenses will lack punch, which is your cue to boost contrast after the shot. Again, shooting RAW files will help, as your image will stand up to editing better. A JPEG will start losing detail if you try to boost contrast too far.

3 CHOOSE YOUR EDITOR CAREFULLY

Some photo editors are non-destructive, which means they don't make changes to your original image file: they simply record the changes you've made in a separate file and leave the original untouched. Other editors, such as Photoshop Elements, alter your original file. In the latter cases, it's best to make a copy of your original file and save it as a TIFF – this way, if you make a mistake your original is still available. You should also beware when working on JPEG files: each time you save them, you lose a small amount of detail as a result of compression.

■ AT-A-GLANCE SETTINGS

SHUTTER SPEED	1/125TH
APERTURE	F/4.9
ISO	250
FOCAL LENGTH	23MM
EXPOSURE	+/-0

Using software such as Adobe Lightroom will enable you to "warm up" underwater images, which can often suffer a cooler white balance.

Using

LENSES

underwater

There's a good reason there are no underwater adapters for telephoto lenses – taking pictures underwater from a distance is all but impossible. Although particles underwater make themselves known most when you use your camera's flash, they're always present, and the more water between you and your subject, the cloudier your shots will be. The best way to take clear, crisp images is to move as close as you can to the things you want to photograph, which is why experienced divers are at a distinct advantage when it comes to underwater photography.

1 LEAVE THE ZOOM ALONE

Whether you're shooting with a compact camera or the kit lens that came with you DSLR, zooming in to get your subject larger in the frame isn't necessarily going to result in a good image. Instead, set your lens to its widest and close the distance between you and what you want to shoot.

2 FOCUS CLOSE

This doesn't mean that longer lenses are out of the question underwater, but you have to use them carefully. Many macro lenses have focal lengths that are nearly telephoto: between 65 and 100mm. The difference between these and a standard long lens is that a macro lens will focus on subjects extremely closely, allowing you to capture minute detail with a bare minimum of water between you and what you're taking a picture of.

3 USING A COMPACT CAMERA

Macro shooting isn't just for DSLRs: many compact cameras have a macro mode that allows closer focusing. To use it, zoom your lens in and look for the flower icon on your camera's menu system. This will allow you to be very close and still able to focus.

▌ AT-A-GLANCE SETTINGS

SHUTTER SPEED	1/110TH
APERTURE	F/3
ISO	50
FOCAL LENGTH	7mm
EXPOSURE	+/-0

Using a macro lens underwater will enable you to focus on your subject closely and capture detailed images.

BACKSCATTER
and underwater lighting

Picture the scene: you're diving on an idyllic reef. From 10ft away, you spot a fascinating fish, zoom your lens in, and fire the shutter. The result? Probably nothing. Even the clearest seawater in the world is chock-full of particles. Tiny grains of sand and minuscule organisms that don't look like much to you will reduce your underwater photographs to murky, cloudy blurs.

▍AT-A-GLANCE SETTINGS

SHUTTER SPEED	1/400TH
APERTURE	F/5
ISO	250
FOCAL LENGTH	6MM
FLASH	ON-CAMERA

1 CLOSE THE DISTANCE

The more distance between you and your subject, the more light-absorbing, particle-filled water your camera has to see through to get a decent picture. This means a longer, blurrier exposure and less chance that the resulting image will be a clear one. If you want to capture sharp images underwater, you need to place yourself less than a metre away from your subject, and ideally be using a wide-angle lens.

2 USING A FLASH

The deeper you go, the more you'll need to augment natural light with a flash or a strobe. Backscatter is a technical term for when a flash hits underwater particles and reflects back into the camera; this will ruin a shot if you're not within touching distance of your subject. Capturing landscape photographs, such as the one above, only come off if you're lucky.

3 IMPROVISE

Adding a flash or strobe to your underwater kit will cost you a fair amount of money, so don't be afraid to improvise with a torch. LED torches are best: they produce extremely bright, neutrally coloured light.

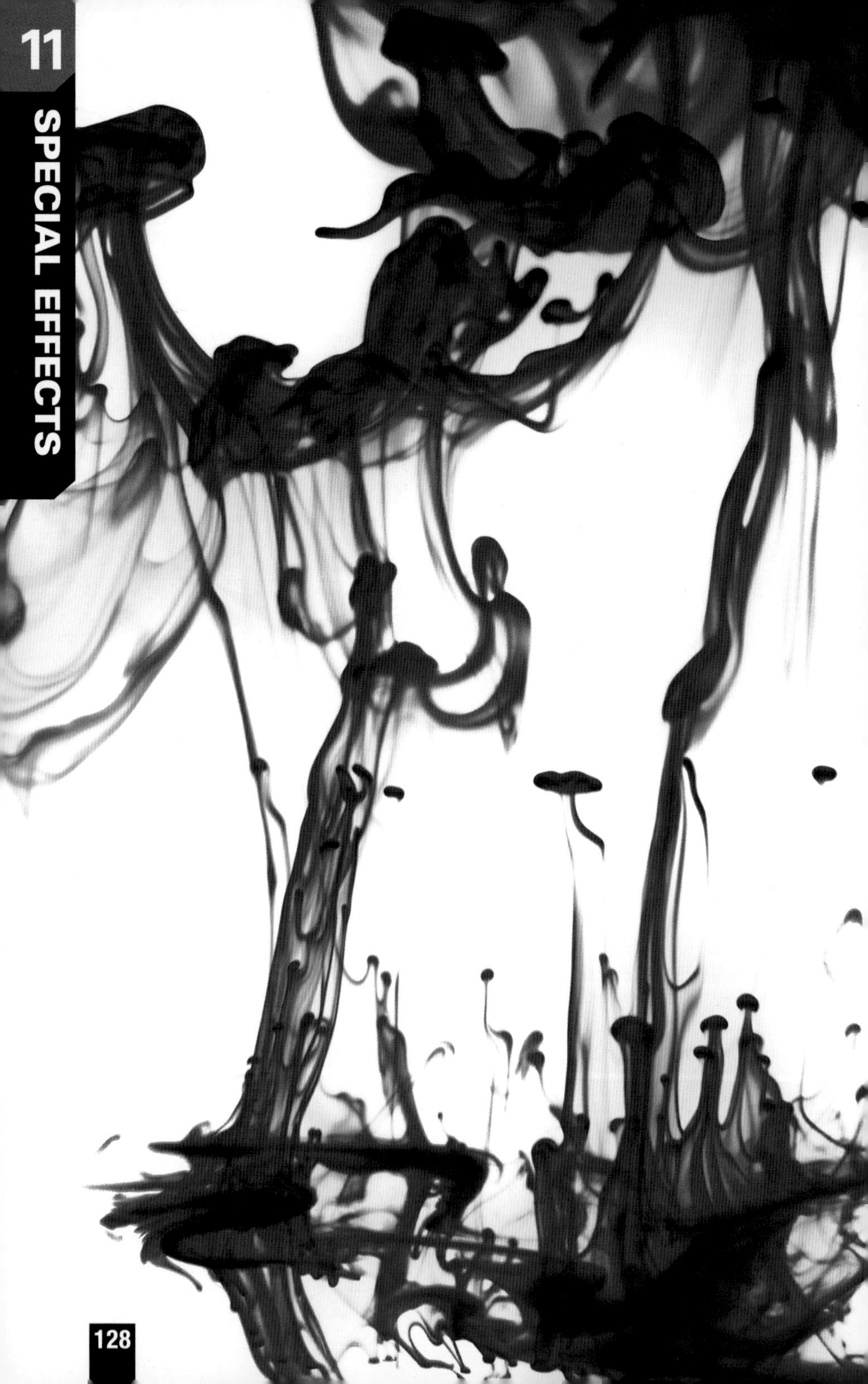

SPECIAL EFFECTS

If you regularly use your camera's fully automatic mode, now's the time to stop. By taking control of settings such as aperture, shutter and ISO, you'll quickly find that your photography becomes less hit and miss, and that the percentage of "keepers" from a day's shoot goes through the roof.

Your camera's manual mode also hides a wealth of creative power. By pairing your camera with decent lights, a macro lens, or a special filter, you can achieve effects that many believe to be the preserve of professionals alone.

The techniques in this section are designed to get you thinking. By the end of p134 (flower close-ups), for instance, you should be able to capture a technically solid macro shot, but it's what you do with the knowledge and the subjects you apply it to, that will determine whether your photos stand out. Likewise, having the ability to freeze in a photo the moment a drop of water hits the surface of liquid in a vase is a nifty trick.

Remember, though, the ideas here are merely starting points for what could be a lifetime of clever, eye-catching photography.

130 In the bag
132 Water droplets
134 Flower close-ups
138 Ink in water
140 Indoor light trails
142 Mist effects on water

IN THE BAG

The list of things that could prove useful for some of the tips in this chapter runs long. Virtually anything can be put to good use, from pipettes for dropping ink (for less than £1) to bunches of flowers and coloured card. More important than owning top-end kit is your own imagination: think of effects you'd like to portray photographically and consider how you might go about making them happen. That said, a few photographic tools will mean your imagination isn't limited by your equipment.

1 EXTERNAL LIGHT

This doesn't necessarily need to be a flash unit; continuous studio lights will work as well. Still, for taking pictures of drops of water, for instance, you'll need a fast shutter speed to freeze the frame, and the only way to achieve that is to use lots of light; it's unlikely simple indoor lighting will suffice. A cable that allows you to fire your flash off-camera is beneficial too.

2 MACRO LENS

Technically, a macro lens is one that produces a 1:1 impression on your camera's sensor, so many lenses with so-called macro modes are really just close-up lenses. Either will be a good step towards getting good depth-of-field effects.

3 CLAMPS

A decent set of these can make setting up complicated shots easier. The Manfrotto clamp (right) is pricey, but it can hold up to 15kg, meaning it can support anything from sheets of backing paper to, well, anything weighing below 15kg. You'll need something strong to hang the clamp itself from.

4 BACKGROUND CARD

It's possible to spend plenty of money on card if you buy the dedicated photographic stuff, but virtually every high street will have a shop that sells good old-fashioned craft paper. Card is better, since it will resist soaking up water as quickly, but scoop up a decent armful of different colours and textures for the most flexibility.

1

2

3

WATER DROPLETS

Taking pictures of water droplets frozen in mid-air is a great way to practise your still-life skills. But you'll need plenty of patience.

1 USE A FLASH

Indoors, your camera will want to set a long shutter speed to ensure a good exposure. That's fine if you're working with something that doesn't move fast (or at all), but to capture falling drops of water you need particularly fast shutter speeds, so you must boost the amount of light with a flash. In this case it's best to buy a hotshoe-mounted, external flash, which is more powerful and effective at higher shutter speeds; internal flashes are often only capable of working at up to 1/200th of a second, but in this instance you need at least four times that.

2 LEARN ABOUT FLASH EXPOSURE COMPENSATION

Your camera's meter – the component that tells it how much light is coming in – is useless here, because you're going to be blasting the flash at your subject. Use manual mode, set your shutter to something fast and open the lens aperture as wide as it will go. Then, use your camera's flash exposure compensation to set a stop of over-exposure. With your camera on a tripod, take a test shot. If you can see your chosen receptacle in the resultant shot, you're ready to go.

3 GET FOCUS PERFECT

Since your lens' aperture is open, depth of field is going to be an issue. This means it's easy to mis-focus and end up with a blurred image. Don't try to focus as you take the shot – by the time your camera drives its focus motor to the right place, the action will have finished. Instead, place something – a ruler, for instance – over whatever is holding your water, and focus on that instead. Turn off autofocus (normally a switch on the lens). Remove the ruler and try to capture the water drops on the place the camera is pre-focused on.

4 FIRE!

Prepare yourself for many outtakes, because this takes perfect timing and a bit of luck. Practise dripping water onto your surface – from a bottle or a tap, for instance – and firing the shutter as the drop falls. With any luck, you should be able to capture the moment the drop hits the surface and breaks into pieces. Since you're working at fast shutter speeds, you don't need to worry about camera shake if you fire the camera by hand.

■ AT-A-GLANCE SETTINGS

SHUTTER SPEED	1/2,000TH
APERTURE	F/5.0
ISO	100
FOCAL LENGTH	190mm
FLASH	OFF-CAMERA

You need a crucial combination of good planning, the right equipment and luck to capture a shot like this.

FLOWER CLOSE-UPS

You'll struggle to find more photogenic subjects than flowers. Vividly coloured with plenty of fascinating, tiny details, they're the perfect way to refine your macro photography. Better yet, they're readily available: virtually every high street in the country has a well-stocked florist, and you only need one example of each type of flower to take a decent close-up. But there are pitfalls. Macro lighting can be difficult, and depth of field is drastically reduced when your lens is so close to your subject. Take your time, though, and before long you'll start turn out spectacular images.

1 LIGHT IS EVERYTHING

With your camera so close to the flower, an onboard flash, or even a hotshoe-mounted flash, is of limited use since the flash is unlikely to be at a useful angle to light your flower evenly. Using a flash cable (around £20) allows you to fire your flash off your camera, while retaining the benefit of its automatic functions. Here, a flash was hung directly above the flower, so the light fired straight down. This produced even lighting without any distracting shadows.

2 THINK MACRO

Macro lenses needn't be hugely expensive, and they allow you to fill the frame even with the smallest of subjects. Some entry-level telephoto lenses have a macro setting that allows you to focus up close while using the lens' longest focal lengths, which is a great way of both filling the frame and saving some cash.

3 FOCUS IS CRITICAL

If you're using an external light you can use a fast shutter setting, so motion blur won't be an issue. But macro lenses have a limited depth of field, so if you don't pay close attention you'll get an out-of-focus shot. To avoid this issue, use a tripod and pre-set your lens' focus. Move the camera backwards or forwards to bring the shot into focus.

■ AT-A-GLANCE SETTINGS

SHUTTER SPEED	1/125TH
APERTURE	F/16
ISO	100
FOCAL LENGTH	190MM
FLASH	MANUAL

Getting up close to a subject requires the right kit, and you'll need to learn how to use it proficiently to get good results.

USING COMPLEMENTARY COLOURS

When you start buying backgrounds for your still-life photography, it's worth getting a decent range of colours, but don't simply buy everything in sight. The principle of complementary colours – colours that look good when placed next to each other – is an important one.

Imagine a wheel of colour, such as the one at **http://kuler.adobe.com**. Colours next to each other will lack contrast, while colours that are opposite each other will appear strong and vibrant. For example, a yellow flower on a red background won't look as good as a blue flower on a yellow background.

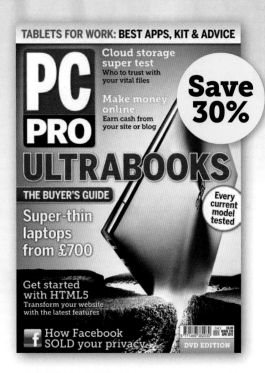

INK IN WATER

You can obtain spectacular results shooting ink as it disperses in water, but it isn't as easy as you'd think. Here's how to master it.

1 DON'T USE FOOD COLOURING

It seems perfect, but in fact food dye disperses far too quickly in water to be of any use. We achieved the result on the right using ink from an ink cartridge designed for use with a fountain pen – it's thick enough that you'll have a minute to get the shot you want. Drip the ink into a clean, large vase filled with water, either straight from the cartridge or with a pipette.

2 PRE-FOCUS

As with photographing water drops (see p132), pre-focusing is the way to go. Place a ruler, lollipop stick or similar object into the water, roughly where you expect to drop the ink. With your focusing tool in place, use your camera's autofocus to bring it into sharp relief. Then, flick the control on your lens to manual focus, and don't touch it again until you're finished.

3 LIGHT THE SCENE

Ink will disperse slowly, so you don't need a flash to freeze the action. However, the more light the better, particularly since this type of photography works best when the background – in our case, a large sheet of white card – is very bright. Being able to use an off-camera flash pointed at the background will be an enormous help. If you don't have one, you might even get away with using a bright white laptop screen.

4 EXPERIMENT

If you do have a flash, use a fast shutter speed and big aperture to get your shots. Drop a small amount of ink into the water and start shooting! You'll get different effects depending whether there's a lot of ink in the water or only a little; you could also find interesting results if you put two drops of ink into the water at once (you may need an assistant for this). The ink will create different shapes every time, so keep going and check your results until you're happy with what you've shot. To create different colours, open your images in almost any image editor and adjust the hue setting to turn the ink from blue to virtually anything else. This is a technique that requires lots of trial and error, but the results are worth it.

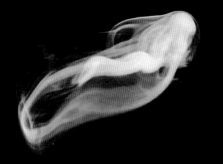

This image was captured using the method described on the left, then attacked in Photoshop. The hue has been changed to a fiery orange, and it's been rotated 180 degrees, giving it a rising, smoke-like effect.

▋ AT-A-GLANCE SETTINGS

SHUTTER SPEED	1/500TH
APERTURE	F/5.6
ISO	100
FOCAL LENGTH	85MM
FLASH	OFF-CAMERA

Indoor
LIGHT TRAILS

Your camera's sensor will record whatever happens in front of it. Normally, you want the sensor exposed for the lowest possible amount of time to minimise blur, but using moving sources of light, such as traffic (see p110), you can create some stunning effects. You don't even need to leave the house: if you have a tripod, a torch and a sense of adventure, you can create the effect pictured opposite in next to no time.

1 MINIMISE EXTERNAL LIGHT

You'll be working with very long shutter speeds here: the picture on the right was taken over 30 seconds, which means plenty of light coming into the sensor. If you don't want to have your background walls hoving into view, make sure the only light in the room is coming from the torch you're painting with. Shoot at night and close the curtains! Remember: anything that stands still for too long could end up in the picture, so make sure your torch-holder keeps moving around to keep them out of the frame.

2 BULB MODE

Setting your camera to a small aperture will allow you to control the amount of light coming in, with the picture here taken at f/22. But even so, most cameras only allow you up to 30 seconds of exposure time, unless they have a bulb mode. The term "bulb" comes from the time when cameras were fired with a rubber ball: squeezing the ball opened the shutter and releasing it closed it. These days, bulb mode means the shutter stays open as long as you hold down the button, giving your "painter" as much or as little time as they need. Use a remote shutter release in this mode, as keeping your finger on the shutter release for an extended period of time will lead to camera shake.

3 TRIPOD

An essential. No lens stabiliser will be able to keep an image sharp for more than a few seconds handheld.

■ AT-A-GLANCE SETTINGS

SHUTTER SPEED	30"
APERTURE	F/22
ISO	100
FOCAL LENGTH	35MM
EXPOSURE	MANUAL, BULB

Long shutter speeds will enable plenty of light to hit the sensor, resulting in stunning effects.

MIST EFFECTS

As we covered on p110 (traffic light trails), understanding motion and being able to portray it in-camera is useful. It works particularly well at night – with little ambient light coming in, it's easy to demonstrate motion with a long shutter speed. It's possible to obtain the same effect during the day, but you need to be clever. With much more light coming into the camera, a long shutter speed will result in a burnt-out, over-exposed image. But with the right kit you'll be able to take some impressive shots.

1 USE A NEUTRAL DENSITY (ND) FILTER

These work in the same way as the graduated filters discussed on p40, but instead of starting dark and fading to clear, they're dark from top to bottom. ND filters are described by the number of stops of light they prevent entering the camera. For example, if you're shooting at f/16 and 1/250th of a second, a ten-stop filter will require you to drop the shutter speed to four seconds to get the same amount of light. This dramatic difference is what will allow you to get both a good exposure and a sensation of movement.

2 THINK ABOUT FRAMING

With very long shutter speeds, you need to be shooting from a steady position, so a tripod is a good option. Try to make the water feature you're shooting – whether it's waves on the sea, a lake or waterfall – as prominent as possible. Remember that clouds move across the sky, so if it looks like a storm is moving in quickly, this is your chance to capture it. The shot on the right works because of the constantly changing lines the water follows, so spend some time hunting for exactly the right spot.

3 THINK BIGGER THAN WATERFALLS!

Shots of blurred moving water can be beautiful, but now you have the kit, think about what else you might use it for. Anything that moves has potential – think cars on a racetrack, or footballers dashing around a pitch. A high vantage point in a busy train station might work equally well. Experimentation is definitely for the best.

This approach is overused on waterfalls, but they're a great place to refine your technique.

■ AT-A-GLANCE SETTINGS

SHUTTER SPEED	1/4TH
APERTURE	F/22
ISO	100
FOCAL DISTANCE	18MM

PRINTING

You could be forgiven for thinking that printing photographs has been consigned to history along with the Model T Ford and the gramophone. But, while sharing images online has immediacy and can reach lots of people fast, printing your work will make it look its very best. There's also a permanence with print that you don't get sharing photos online: you'll need to be at your best both behind the camera and in front of the computer to create prints that stand the test of time and look great on a wall.

As ever, life isn't as simple as buying a printer and instantly whirring out perfect prints. There are all kinds of things to consider, from paper and ink choices to the option of outsourcing your printing to either a mass-market online printer or a more bespoke, fine-art outfit. Along the way you'll need to consider your ink, paper and finishing, and you'll need to have print in mind throughout your photographic process. You can get away with a surprising amount when looking at photos on a computer screen. Printing of any kind is far less forgiving in terms of detail, exposure and the kinds of lens defects you might overlook if your photography is digital-only.

As ever, help is at hand. Read on to find out all you could want to know about amateur and professional printing. By the end of the chapter, you'll be turning out museum-quality prints.

146 How to choose your printer

148 Understanding inks

150 Understanding paper

152 Processing your image

154 Cropping & resolution

156 Professional printing

158 Framing & mounting

How to choose your printer

Printing from home has undeniable benefits – chiefly convenience, but there are benefits for perfectionists, too. If a print comes out from your home printer with skewed colours or imperfect composition, getting it re-done takes only minutes.

A4 vs A3

Decent A4 printers can cost around £140, but with DSLRs capable of enormous images, it's worth investigating an A3 or A3+ printer. That way, when you find a belting shot you can print it nearly a foot and a half long without leaving your house. Expect to pay £400 for a good-quality model, and plenty more for ink. The results can be surprisingly good value if you print a lot – more so if you can find fans willing to pay for your work.

PERILS OF A SUPERMARKET MFD

Bargain multifunction devices (MFDs) routinely cost less than £50, and as jacks-of-all-trades devices they're good, but they're less well-suited for doing your finely crafted photos justice. Cheap printers generally offer only a few ink tanks (see p148), meaning the number of colours they can produce (their colour gamut) is restricted. If you want to print photos, and have a printer capable of handling all types of paper and card, you'll need to spend a little more.

Paying for the printer itself is only half the story: bear in mind ink and paper costs for the full picture.

WHAT TO LOOK FOR – AND HOW MUCH TO PAY

You can become sidetracked by all kinds of bells and whistles when looking for a printer, but the best way to choose one is to read professional reviews. Computer magazines and high-end photography titles provide a wealth of information and professionally test devices. Expect to pay around £140 for a solid A4 printer. Features such as networking or a memory card reader will cost extra, but image quality is the main concern.

A WORD ABOUT RUNNING COSTS

Individual ink cartridges might only cost a tenner, but if your printer takes eight ink tanks you're in for some big bills when they need replacing. Paper is a similar story: standard, glossy paper is reasonably affordable, but upgrading to the good stuff, such as Epson's museum-grade paper, could cost up to £5 per page. Unless you're expecting to churn out dozens of prints, it's worth considering a professional print shop before lightening your wallet.

Understanding inks

In all likelihood, any printer you buy for your home will be an inkjet: it's by far the most popular consumer printing technology, and it sees plenty of use with professionals as well. But it's a complicated, automatic chemistry set, and knowing what's going on under the cover is a good way to get the best out of it.

HOW DOES IT WORK?

As the name suggests, an inkjet creates an image by firing tiny drops of ink (around the diameter of a human hair) at a sheet of paper. These drops are absorbed by the page to create an image. The reaction between the paper and the ink is a complicated one that printer manufacturers spend millions developing, in the name of improved image quality and longer-lasting prints.

WHAT DO EXTRA INKS DO?

Cheaper inkjets come with two ink tanks: one black cartridge, and one cartridge containing cyan, magenta and yellow inks. Between them, they can create a wide range of colours. However, expensive printers allow you to use more inks – for example, replacing the black ink cartridge with a secondary colour cartridge. Adding a red ink tank will enable a printer to create a broader

CMYK cartridges mix colours to produce images: some printers have more tanks for a wider colour gamut.

range of skin tones. It's all about increasing the size of the printer's colour gamut – the maximum number of colours the printer can produce.

ARE THIRD-PARTY INKS WORTH THE RISK?

As soon as you've paid for your new printer, you'll start noticing adverts for third-party inks. These inks are far cheaper than manufacturer-made inks, but manufacturers discourage you from using them. This is partly protectionism – companies such as Epson and HP spend millions developing ink – but there are practical concerns too: it's impossible to guarantee that a particular brand of third-party ink will work perfectly with your printer. This is less of a concern if you're printing the occasional web page and letter to the bank, but for colour-critical photo printing, the manufacturer's recommended inks are the best bet, for both reliability and quality.

Forget supermarket
gloss prints:
investigate the full
range of paper
options your printer
supports for more
striking images.

Understanding paper

You'll be amazed at the difference changing the paper your prints are made on can make. Whether you print at home or using a professional outlet, now is the time to get away from simply churning out prints on reflective glossy paper.

WHAT DOES IT ALL MEAN?

Different paper absorbs ink differently, and that can result in radically different effects when printing. Glossy paper is great for printing photos that have had minimal editing work: it makes colours seem bolder and adds contrast to images. But it isn't a terribly subtle medium. Also, once you've added a little saturation to the colours in your images, glossy paper can seem like overkill. Instead, investigate printing on matte or even photorag paper: the latter has a rough, almost unfinished texture that makes properly finished prints look like works of art. High-end semi-gloss papers are a good intermediate option. For those looking to make a real statement, Kodak even makes a metallic-finish paper.

ARE THIRD-PARTY PAPERS WORTH IT?

Unlike third-party inks, the answer here is "undoubtedly". It's certainly worth investigating the paper your printer manufacturer can supply: some, such as Epson and Canon, make a wide range of papers ranging from gloss to semi-gloss (perfect for holiday snaps) and photorag papers. But there are lots of players in the fine-art printing industry, and it's worth seeing what the likes of Hahnemuhle or Harman have to offer. Outfits such as **www.theprintspace.co.uk** offer sample packs so you can investigate your options before splashing out. A word of warning: consumer printers have a maximum paper weight they can run through their mechanisms, measured in GSM (grams per square metre). High-end photo paper will be far heavier than standard office A4 or normal glossy paper, so check what your printer can handle before jamming it up with museum-grade paper.

Processing your image for print

Processing an image to share online is easy: with the quality of other people's monitors varying so widely, you can get away with all kinds of sins. And, with many people arriving at images via tiny thumbnails, pictures with ultra-high contrast stand a better chance of being noticed. Preparing an image for print is an altogether more subtle art.

WHAT TO LOOK FOR IN AN IMAGE

Images for printing don't need to be perfect out of the camera, but the best possible quality before your shot has been processed doesn't hurt. Remember that certain things, such as poor focusing or camera shake resulting in blurry images, are impossible to fix when editing, so don't waste time attempting to save shaky exposures. Under- or over-exposed shots can often be corrected, but the more you need to darken or brighten an image, the more detail you'll lose in the editing process. For that reason, put in the effort behind the camera to get your images right at the point of capture.

CHECKING SHARPNESS

Viewing images in their entirety is a good way to check exposure and composition, but viewing images zoomed-out means every

Zooming this image to 100% shows that it's nearly perfectly sharp, and therefore a great candidate for printing.

now and then you'll send something to print that could be sharper. Softness in images is distracting: the best way to check is to zoom in to 100%. If the image doesn't look crisp and detailed, it won't look its best as a large-scale print.

PROCESSING: A LITTLE GOES A LONG WAY

If you've got into the habit of aggressively thrusting the adjustment sliders around in your chosen editing software, now's the time to stop. Print is very unforgiving to clumsy editing, and images with over-exuberant colours, heavy-handed sharpening and fake vignetting in the corners look their worst when printed large.

Cropping & resolution

In recent years, the megapixel count on a camera has become less important. The majority of cameras less than five years old have enough pixels to create huge (A2 and often even larger) images. However, if you start cropping your images, you may find that your shots are too small to print at large sizes. Here's how to do the maths to avoid surprises.

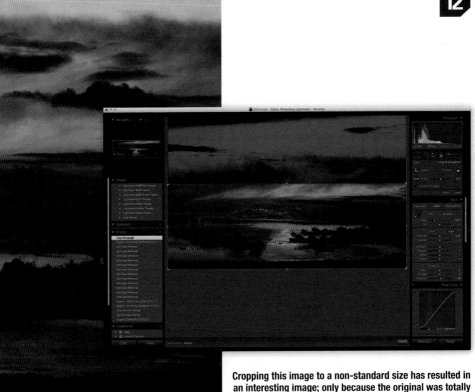

Cropping this image to a non-standard size has resulted in an interesting image; only because the original was totally sharp is it still a candidate for printing.

WORKING OUT PRINT SIZES

To work out how big you can print an image, without needing to enlarge it in software, apply some simple maths. Multiply the number of pixels on the long edge and divide it by 300; 300 being the normal number of dots per inch contained in a high-quality photo print. For example, an 8-megapixel image is 3,456 pixels across – divide by 300 and you get 11.52. The resulting number is the maximum number of inches your image can be in width. If your desired print size is shorter, the image will fit comfortably; if it's larger, you'll need to interpolate the image to add pixels to get it to fit. As you'll notice, modern DSLRs produce very large images, which means they'll still print well after cropping.

WHAT IS INTERPOLATION?

Interpolation adds pixels to an image by estimating what the image would look like if it was enlarged. It's particularly useful if you crop an image but want to print at larger sizes. As it involves estimation, interpolated images tend not to look as good as full-scale images – nonetheless, you'll be surprised how good they can look, even when blown up. The most crucial factor is the sharpness of the original: if there's a hint of softness, avoid cropping at all. It's possible to buy plugins for applications such as Photoshop, Lightroom and Aperture that claim to offer superlative image quality when upscaling images – it's worth investigating free trials of software such as Perfect Resize 7 to put those claims to the test.

Printing professionally

Home printing is the most convenient way to produce hard copies of your images. However, by the time you've bought a printer and worked out your per-page costs, you may find that professional printing is the more economical option – and that isn't the only benefit.

WHY PRINT PROFESSIONALLY?

Apart from the economic side (expect to pay around £10 for an A3 print), there are other benefits to professional printing. For example, becoming a fluent photographer takes work; learning how to print to a professional standard is yet another skill to learn and perfect. Using a professional printer is a little like using a professional mechanic; you can lean on someone else's skill and experience while you concentrate on something else. Professional printers own professional kit, which means you can print at strange or huge sizes without needing to invest personally. A professional printer will also hold a choice of papers and finishes, so you won't have to buy a whole pack of fine-art paper simply to experiment.

CHOOSING AND TESTING YOUR PRINTER

Before spending big sums on prints, it makes sense to first put your chosen printer to the test. Some high-end outfits, such as **www. printspace.co.uk**, provide printer profiles for you to use in your editing software, so you can see approximately how your images will print. Others, such as **www.photobox. co.uk**, supply a colour-matching card with your order so you can adapt monitor settings to their printers. The practical approach is to order a few medium-sized prints to see how they turn out.

MONITOR CALIBRATION

If you're serious about creating top-quality prints, calibrating your monitor is essential. This involves using a small

hardware device to set your monitor's brightness and contrast settings to known values. Hardware calibrators can cost as little as £50, and will make editing and printing your images far more reliable.

Professional printers inevitably take longer to deliver than printing from home, but they're a good option economically – and will offer more options.

Framing & mounting

Printing your shots at impressive sizes isn't the end of the job: if your lovingly crafted prints are left to collect dust in a drawer, you've missed the point.

PROFESSIONAL FRAMING

It's possible to get professional results by framing your prints yourself. Everyone's favourite Swedish furniture maker does a surprisingly decent range of photo frames, and with a bit of framing tape (stocked at most arts and crafts shops) you can create a good-looking finished product. However, for a piece of long-lasting furniture, consider paying more for a custom-built frame. The chief benefit, apart from build quality, is that you can specify exact dimensions, allowing you to use whatever paper size or crop size you choose. Expect to pay around £30 for a basic A3 frame.

BACKING IMAGES

Mounting your images is another way to give them a bit of added protection. For example, the foamboard supplied by most arts and crafts stores can be used as a lightweight backing for prints, and the result can be surprisingly professional if you use high-quality spray adhesive and a sharp art scalpel to create a custom finish. Foam-backed images are also extremely light, which makes them ideal for mounting on walls you're reluctant to drive nails into. Professional printers often offer mounting services – for an A3 image professionally mounted on card, you'll pay just less than £20, including the print.

BORDERS

It's unlikely you add borders to your images as a matter of course, but it's worth considering when creating an image for mounting on a wall. Most frames will have a cardboard matte included anyway, so any print you create will need an area of dead space to allow you to fix the matte to the print. Borders can add a touch of arty class to most prints, and can be achieved in minutes in most photo editors.

Adding borders to an image is a quick and easy
way to create an eye-catching print.

Glossary

APERTURE The opening in the lens that admits light. An aperture can be adjusted to admit more or less light.

APERTURE PRIORITY A camera mode in which the user sets aperture size, and the camera adjusts shutter speed.

ARTIFACTS Compressed images show blockiness. Frequently saving a JPEG can make these artifacts more obvious.

AUTOFOCUS The process through which your camera detects the distance between it and a subject, and drives the lens to bring the subject into focus on the sensor.

BRACKETING A feature on most DSLRs in which the camera shoots one "correct" exposure, then one brighter and one darker to increase the chances of getting an accurate image.

BUFFER A camera's internal memory, which fills up as you shoot in continuous mode. Images are cleared from the buffer onto a memory card.

BULB An exposure mode in which the camera's shutter remains open until your release the shutter button.

CHROMATIC ABERRATION The purple fringing that occurs on areas of high contrast in some images. More expensive lenses suffer from this less than cheap lenses.

CONTINUOUS SHOOTING A mode in which pictures are captured sequentially for as long as you hold down the shutter button.

CONTRAST The difference in the range of brightness between light and dark areas of an image.

DEPTH OF FIELD When an image has one area that appears sharply focused, with other areas out of focus.

DSLR (Digital Single Lens Reflex) A digital camera with an optical viewfinder and mechanical mirror system.

EXIF (EXchangeable Image Format) Data collected with each image you shoot, typically including shutter speed, aperture and the date and time.

EXPOSURE COMPENSATION The ability to force your camera to shoot a brighter or darker exposure than it thinks it should.

F-STOP The (now antiquated) mechanism used to set a lens' aperture. "Stop" is now used to denote changes in shutter speed, aperture size and ISO setting.

HOT-SHOE The metal bracket on top of all DSLRs. Designed to accept and send data to a flashgun; some microphones fit as well.

ISO A measure of a camera's light sensitivity. The higher the ISO, the more the sensor reacts to light. High ISO result in images with more noise.

JPEG By far the most common image format. All DSLRs shoot JPEGs, although RAW files gather more data in a larger file.

LCD The technology used on the majority of DSLR preview monitors.

LENS The glass optic used to focus light onto a camera's sensor. On a DSLR, the lens can be removed and exchanged for different lenses.

LOSSY A way of describing a file format that saves hard disk space through compressing and sacrificing detail.

MACRO A technique that produces an image on a sensor that is actual size.

METERING The method a camera uses to determine the appropriate automatic exposure for a scene.

RAW An unprocessed file captured by a DSLR. These files contain more detail than JPEGs, but they take up more disk space.

RESOLUTION A way of describing how many individual dots an image is made up from. A higher resolution results in larger file sizes.

SENSOR The microchip in a camera that reacts to light, allowing an image to be made.

SHUTTER The mechanism in front of a camera's sensor. It moves to allow an image to be captured when the shutter release button is pressed.

STABILISATION Compensating for the movement of a camera during an exposure, either by moving elements in the lens or the camera sensor.

TELEPHOTO Technically, any lens that has a focal length longer than its physical length. Practically, lenses longer than 150mm are normally considered telephoto.

VIGNETTING An effect by which the corners of a frame are darkened.

WHITE BALANCE A camera's way of detecting the light source in a frame, and setting the white point appropriately to produce accurate colours.